Say it in

SPANISH

LEON J. COHEN
Goshen Central School
Goshen, N.Y.

and A. C. ROGERS

DOVER PUBLICATIONS, INC.

NEW YORK

Published in Canada by General Publishing Company, Ltd., 30 Lesmill Road, Don Mills, Toronto, Ontario.

Published in the United Kingdom by Constable and Company, Ltd., 10 Orange Street, London WC 2.

Standard Book Number: 486-20811-7
Library of Congress Catalog Card Number: 56-20451

Manufactured in the United States of America
Dover Publications, Inc.
180 Varick Street
New York, N. Y. 10014

CONTENTS

SCHEME OF PRONUNCIATION

The difficulties of pronunciation of Spanish for an American arise mainly from the difference in the pronunciation of vowels. English vowels are usually not one sound, but two; Spanish vowels are pure, consisting of one sound only. Remember not to drawl them as in English.

The pronunciation given should be read simply as in English, with the stress placed upon the syllables in capital letters. Since in some cases the pronunciation of a group of letters differs according to the English word in which it is found and since a few Spanish sounds cannot be represented in English, the following rules should be remembered:

A or *AH*—a broad *a* as in *hard.*

AY—as in *say.*

EE—as in *bee.*

GH—as the *g* in *go.*

H—as in *home,* with the *H* breathed vigorously.

O or *OH*—as in *no.*

OO—as in *moon.*

R—flip tongue against gums of upper front teeth, as in a Scotsman's burr.

RR—a more strongly rolled *R* sound.

SYOHN—as in *see OWN.*

KYAY—as in *key A.*

TYAY—as in *tea A.*

Although there are some regional differences, if you follow the pronunciation given in this book, you will be understood wherever Spanish is spoken.

NOTE. For easy reference, all items are indexed by item number. In order to facilitate revision of this book, a few numbers have been skipped between major divisions. These interruptions in the consecutive numbering of the entries do not indicate omissions of any part of the text.

USEFUL EXPRESSIONS

EXPRESIONES UTILES

1. Yes.   No.   Perhaps.
Sí.   No.   Puede ser.
see.   no.   PWAY-day sayr.

2. Please ——.
Haga el favor de ——.
AH-gah el fah-VOR day ——.

3. Excuse me.
Dispénseme.
deess-PEN-say-may.

4. Thanks (very much).
(Muchas) gracias.
(MOO-chahss) GRAH-syahss.

5. You are welcome.
No hay de que.
no I day kay.

6. Do you speak English?
¿Habla usted inglés?
AH-bla oos-TED een-GLAYSS?

7. I speak only English (French).
Sólo hablo inglés (francés).
SO-lo AH-blo een-GLAYSS (frahn-SAYSS).

8. German, Italian.
Alemán, italiano.
ah-lay-MAHN, ee-tah-LYAH-no.

9. I am from the United States.
Soy de los Estados Unidos.
soy day lohss ess-TA-dohss oo-NEE-dohss.

10. My (mailing) address is ——.
Mi dirección (para cartas) es ——.
mee dee-rek-SYOHN (PA-rah KAR-tahss) ess ——.

11. He (she) is from ——.
Él (ella) es de ——.
el (AY-yah) ess day ——.

12. Please speak more slowly.
Favor de hablar más despacio.
fah-VOR day ah-BLAHR mahss dess-PA-syo.

13. I (do not) understand.
(No) comprendo.
(no) kohm-PREN-doh.

14. Repeat it, please.
Favor de repetirlo.
fah-VOR day rray-pay-TEER-lo.

15. Again. Otra vez. *O-tra vess.*

16. Write it down, please.
Escríbalo, por favor.
ess-KREE-ba-lo, por fah-VOR.

17. What do you wish?
¿Qué desea usted?
kay day-SAY-ah oos-TED?

18. How much (is it)?
¿Cuánto (es)?
KWAN-toh (ess)?

19. Come here. Come in.
Venga acá. Pase usted.
VEN-gah ah-KA. PA-say oos-TED.

20. Wait a moment.
Espere un momento.
ess-PAY-ray oon mo-MEN-toh.

21. Why? When?
¿Por qué? ¿Cuándo?
por KAY? KWAN-doh?

22. How? How long?
¿Cómo? ¿Cuánto tiempo?
KO-mo? KWAN-toh TYEM-po?

23. Who? What?
¿Quién? ¿Qué?
kyen? kay?

24. Where is ——?
¿Dónde está ——?
DOHN-day ess-TA ——?

25. Ladies' Room.
Damas *or* Señoras *or* Mujeres.
DA-mahss or *say-NYO-rahss* or *moo-HAY-ress.*

26. Men's Room.
Caballeros *or* Señores *or* Hombres.
ka-ba-YAY-rohss or *say-NYO-ress* or *OHM-bress.*

27. Here, there.
Aquí, allí.
ah-KEE, ah-YEE.

28. It is (not) all right.
(No) está bien.
(no) ess-TA byen.

29. It is old (new).
Es viejo (nuevo).
ess VYAY-ho (NWAY-vo).

30. Empty, full.
Vacío, lleno.
vah-SEE-o, YAY-no.

31. That is (not) all.
Eso (no) es todo.
AY-so (no) ess TOH-doh.

32. To, from, with.
A, de, con.
ah, day, kohn.

33. In, on, near, far.
En, sobre, cerca de, lejos de.
en, SO-bray, SAYR-ka day, LAY-hohss day.

34. In front of, behind.
Enfrente de, detrás de.
en-FREN-tay day, day-TRAHSS day.

35. Beside, inside, outside.
Al lado de, dentro de, fuera de.
ahl LA-doh day, DEN-tro day, FWAY-rah day.

36. Something, nothing.
Algo, nada.
AHL-go, NA-da.

37. Several, few.
Algunos, pocos.
ahl-GOO-nohss, PO-kohss.

38. More, less.
Más, menos.
mahss, MAY-nohss.

39. A little.
Un poquito de.
oon po-KEE-toh day.

40. Enough, too much.
Suficiente, demasiado.
soo-fee-SYEN-tay, day-ma-SYAH-doh.

41. Much, many.
Mucho, muchos.
MOO-cho, MOO-chohss.

42. Good, better (than).
Bueno, mejor (que).
BWAY-no, may-HOR (kay).

43. Bad, worse (than).
Malo, peor (que).
MA-lo, pay- OR (kay).

44. Now, immediately.
Ahora, en seguida.
ah-O-rah, en say-GHEE-da.

45. Soon, later.
Pronto, más tarde.
PROHN-toh, mahss TAR-day.

46. As soon as possible.
Lo más pronto posible.
lo mahss PROHN-toh po-SEE-blay.

47. At the latest.
A más tardar.
ah mahss tar-DAHR.

48. At least.
Por lo menos.
por lo MAY-nohss.

49. It is (too) late.
Es (muy) tarde.
ess (mwee) TAR-day.

50. It is early.
Es temprano.
ess tem-PRAH-no.

51. Slowly, slower.
Despacio, más despacio.
dess-PA-syo, mahss dess-PA-syo.

52. Quickly, faster.
Aprisa, más aprisa.
ah-PREE-sah, mahss ah-PREE-sah.

53. I am (not) in a hurry.
(No) tengo prisa.
(no) TEN-go PREE-sah.

54. I am warm (cold).
Tengo calor (frío).
TEN-go ka-LOHR (FREE-o).

55. Hungry, thirsty, sleepy.
Hambre, sed, sueño.
AHM-bray, sed, SWAY-nyo.

56. I am busy (tired, ill).
Estoy ocupado (cansado, enfermo).
ess-TOY o-koo-PA-doh (kahn-SAH-doh, en-FAYR-mo).

57. What is the matter here?
¿Qué pasa aquí?
kay PA-sah ah-KEE?

58. Help! Fire! Thief!
¡Socorro! ¡Fuego! ¡Ladrón!
so-KO-rro! FWAY-go! la-DROHN!

59. Look out! ¡Cuidado! *kwee-DA-doh!*

60. Listen. Look here.
Oiga. Mire.
OY-gah. MEE-ray.

61. Can you help (tell) me?

¿Puede usted ayudarme (decirme)?

PWAY-day oos-TED ah-yoo-DAHR-may (day-SEER-may)?

62. I am looking for ——.

Busco ——.

BOOS-ko ——.

63. I should like ——.

Quisiera ——.

kee-SYAY-rah ——.

64. Can you recommend a ——?

¿Puede usted recomendar un ——?

PWAY-day oos-TED rray-ko-men-DAHR oon ——?

65. Do you want ——?

¿Desea usted ——?

day-SAY-ah oos-TED ——?

66. I am (very) glad.

Me alegro (mucho).

may ah-LAY-gro (MOO-cho).

67. I am sorry.

Lo siento.

lo SYEN-toh.

68. It is (not) my fault.

(No) es mi culpa.

(no) ess mee KOOL-pa.

69. Whose fault is it?

¿Quién tiene la culpa?

kyen TYAY-nay la KOOL-pa?

70. I (do not) know.

(No) sé.

(no) say.

71. I (do not) think so.
Creo que sí (no).
KRAY-o kay see (no).

72. What is that for?
¿Para qué es eso?
PA-rah kay ess AY-so?

73. What is this called in Spanish?
¿Cómo se llama esto en español?
KO-mo say YAH-ma ESS-toh en ess-pa-NYOHL?

74. How do you say ——?
¿Cómo se dice ——?
KO-mo say DEE-say ——?

75. How do you spell 'antiguo'?
¿Cómo se deletrea 'antiguo'?
KO-mo say day-lay-TRAY-ah ahn-TEE-gwo?

DIFFICULTIES   LAS DIFICULTADES

80. I cannot find my hotel address.
No puedo hallar la dirección de mi hotel.
no PWAY-doh ah-YAHR la dee-rek-SYOHN day mee o-TELL.

81. I do not remember the street.
No recuerdo cómo se llama la calle.
no rray-KWAYR-doh KO-mo say YAH-ma la KA-yay.

82. I have lost my friends.
No encuentro a mis amigos.
no en-KWEN-tro ah meess ah-MEE-gohss.

83. I left my purse (wallet) in ——.
Dejé mi bolsa (mi cartera) en ——.
*day-HAY mee BOHL-sah (mee kar-TAY-rah)
en ——.*

84. I forgot my money (key).
Olvidé mi dinero (llave).
ohl-vee-DAY mee dee-NAY-ro (YAH-vay).

85. I have missed my train (plane).
He perdido mi tren (avión).
ay payr-DEE-doh mee tren (ahv-YOHN).

86. What am I to do?
¿Qué debo hacer?
kay DAY-bo ah-SAYR?

87. You said it would cost ——.
Usted dijo que costaría ——.
oos-TED DEE-ho kay kohss-ta-REE-ah ——.

88. They are bothering me (us).
Ellos me (nos) molestan.
AY-yohss may (nohss) mo-LESS-tahn.

89. Go away.
Váyase.
VAH-yah-say.

90. I will call a policeman.
Llamaré un policía.
yah-ma-RAY oon po-lee-SEE-ah.

91. I have been robbed of ——.
Me han robado ——.
may ahn rro-BA-doh ———.

92. Where is the police station?

¿Dónde está la estación de policía?
DOHN-day ess-TA la ess-ta-SYOHN day po-lee-SEE-ah?

93. The Lost and Found Desk.

La sección de objetos perdidos.
la sek-SYOHN day ohb-HAY-tohss payr-DEE-dohss.

GREETINGS, INTRODUCTIONS, ETC.

SALUDOS, PRESENTACIONES, ETC.

98. Good morning *or* **Good day.**

Buenos días.
BWAY-nohss DEE-ahss.

99. Good afternoon.

Buenas tardes.
BWAY-nahss TAR-dess.

100. Good evening *or* **Good night.**

Buenas noches.
BWAY-nahss NO-chess.

101. Good-bye.   Until next time.

Adiós.   Hasta la próxima vez.
ah-DYOHSS.   AHSS-ta la PROHK-see-ma vess.

102. My name is ——.

Me llamo ——.
may YAH-mo ——.

103. What is your name?

¿Cómo se llama usted?
KO-mo say YAH-ma oos-TED?

104. May I introduce Mr. ——, Mrs. ——, Miss ——?

¿Permítame presentar ai señor ——, a la señora ——, a la señorita ——?

payr-MEE-ta-may pray-sen-TAR ahl say-NYOR ——, ah la say-NYO-rah ——, ah la say-nyo-REE-ta ——?

105. My wife, my husband.

Mi esposa, mi esposo *or* mi marido.
mee ess-PO-sah, mee ess-PO-so or mee ma-REE-doh.

106. My daughter, my son.

Mi hija, mi hijo.
mee EE-ha, mee EE-ho.

107. My friend.

Mi amigo *or* mi amiga.
mee ah-MEE-go or mee ah-MEE-gah.

108. My sister, my brothers.

Mi hermana, mis hermanos.
mee ayr-MA-na, meess ayr-MA-nohss.

109. I am very glad to meet you.

Me alegro de conocerle *or less formally* Mucho gusto.
may ah-LAY-gro day ko-no-SAYR-lay or MOO-cho GOOSS-toh.

110. The pleasure is mine.

Igualmente.
ee-gwahl-MEN-tay.

111. How are you?

¿Cómo está usted?
KO-mo ess-TA oos-TED?

112. Fine, thanks.   And you?

Muy bien, gracias. ¿Y usted?
mwee byen, GRAH-syahss.   ee oos-TED?

113. How is your family?

¿Cómo está su familia?
KO-mo ess-TA soo fah-MEE-lyah?

114. (Not) very well, thanks.

(No) muy bien, gracias.
(no) mwee byen, GRAH-syahss.

115. Please sit down.

Haga el favor de sentarse.
AH-gah el fah-VOR day sen-TAR-say.

116. I have enjoyed myself very much.

Me he divertido mucho.
may ay dee-vayr-TEE-doh MOO-cho.

117. I hope to see you again (soon).

Espero verle otra vez (pronto).
ess-PAY-ro VAYR-lay O-tra vess (PROHN-toh).

118. Come to see me (to see us).

Venga usted a verme (vernos).

VEN-gah oos-TED ah VAYR-may (VAYR-nohss).

119. Are you free this afternoon (this evening)?

¿Está usted libre esta tarde (esta noche)?

ess-TA oos-TED LEE-bray ESS-ta TAR-day (ESS-ta NO-chay)?

120. Please give me your address.

Haga el favor de darme su dirección.

AH-gah el fah-VOR day DAHR-may soo dee-rek-SYOHN.

121. Give my (our) regards to ——.

Dé mis (nuestros) recuerdos a ——.

day meess (NWESS-trohss) rray-KWAYR-dohss ah ——.

122. I am (We are) going to ——.

Voy (Vamos) a ——.

voy (VAH-mohss) ah ——.

TRAVEL. General Expressions

EL VIAJE. Expresiones generales

129. I want to go to the airline office.

Quiero ir a la oficina de la línea aérea.

KYAY-ro eer ah la o-fee-SEE-na day la LEE-nay-ah ah-AY-ray-ah.

130. Where is ——?

¿Dónde está ——?

DOHN-day ess-TA ——?

131. The airport.
El aeropuerto.
el ah-ay-ro-PWAYR-toh.

132. The bus station.
La estación de autobuses.
la ess-ta-SYOHN day out-o-BOO-sess.

133. The dock.
El muelle.
el MWAY-yay.

134. The railroad station.
La estación de ferrocarriles.
la ess-ta-SYOHN day fay-rro-ka-RREE-less.

135. The ticket office.
La taquilla.
la ta-KEE-yah.

136. A ticket, a timetable.
Un billete, un horario.
oon bee-YAY-tay, oon o-RAH-ryo.

137. A porter.
Un mozo.
oon MO-so.

138. The baggage room.
La sala de equipajes.
la SAH-la day ay-kee-PA-hess.

139. The platform.
El andén.
el ahn-DEN.

140. How does one go?
¿Por dónde se va?
por DOHN-day say vah?

141. When will we arrive at ——?

¿Cuándo llegaremos a ——?
KWAHN-doh yay-gah-RAY-mohss ah ——?

142. Please get me a taxi.

Haga el favor de llamarme un taxi.
AH-gah el fah-VOR day yah-MAR-may oon TAHK-see.

143. Is this seat taken?

¿Está reservado este asiento?
ess-TA rray-sayr-VAH-doh ESS-tay ah-SYEN-toh?

144. Can I reserve a (front) seat?

¿Puedo reservar un asiento (delantero)?
PWAY-doh rray-sayr-VAHR oon ah-SYEN-toh (day-lahn-TAY-ro)?

145. A seat by the window.

Un asiento junto a la ventana.
oon ah-SYEN-toh HOON-toh ah la ven-TA-na.

146. Is this the (direct) way to ——?

¿Es éste el camino (directo) a ——?
ess ESS-tay el ka-MEE-no (dee-REK-toh) ah ——?

147. How long will it take to go?

¿En cuánto tiempo se llega?
en KWAHN-toh TYEM-po say YAY-gah?

148. Where do I turn?

¿Dónde doy vuelta?
DOHN-day doy VWELL-ta?

149. To the north, south.
Al norte, al sur.
ahl NOR-tay, ahl soor.

150. From the east, west.
Del este, del oeste.
del ESS-tay, del o-ESS-tay.

151. Straight ahead.
Adelante.
ah-day-LAHN-tay.

152. To the left (right).
A la izquierda (la derecha).
ah la eess-KYAYR-dah (la day-RAY-cha).

153. Forward, back.
Adelante, atrás.
ah-day-LAHN-tay, ah-TRAHSS.

154. What street is this?
¿Qué calle es ésta?
kay KA-yay ess ESS-ta?

155. Circle, place, square.
El círculo, el parque, la plaza.
el SEER-koo-lo, el PAR-kay, la PLAH-sah.

156. Two blocks ahead.
Dos cuadras de frente.
dohss KWAH-drahss day FREN-tay.

157. Please point.
Sírvase indicar.
SEER-vah-say een-dee-kar.

158. Do I have to change?
¿Tengo que cambiar?
TEN-go kay kahm-BYAHR?

159. Please tell me where to get off.
Por favor, avíseme dónde me bajo.
*por fah-VOR, ah-VEE-say-may DOHN-day may
BA-ho.*

At the Customs

La aduana

162. Where is the customs?
¿Dónde está la aduana?
DOHN-day ess-TA la ah-DWAH-na?

163. This is my baggage. —— pieces.
Éste es mi equipaje. —— piezas.
*ESS-tay ess mee ay-kee-PA-hay. —— PYAY-
sahss.*

164. Here is my permit (passport).
Aquí tiene usted mi permiso (pasaporte).
*ah-KEE TYAY-nay oos-TED mee payr-MEE-so
(pa-sah-POR-tay).*

165. Shall I open everything?
¿Debo abrir todo?
DAY-bo ah-BREER TOH-doh?

166. I cannot open that.
No puedo abrir ése.
no PWAY-doh ah-BREER AY-say.

167. I have lost the key.
Perdí la llave.
payr-DEE la YAH-vay.

168. I have nothing to declare (for sale).
No tengo nada que declarar (para vender).
*no TEN-go NA-da kay day-klah-RAHR (PA-rah
ven-DAYR).*

169. All this is for my personal use.

Todo esto es para mi uso personal.
TOH-doh ESS-toh ess PA-rah mee OO-so payr-so-NAHL.

170. There is nothing here but ——.

No hay más que —— aquí.
no I mahss kay —— ah-KEE.

171. These are gifts.

Éstos son regalos.
ESS-tohss sohn rray-GAH-lohss.

172. Are these things dutiable?

¿Hay que pagar impuestos sobre estos artículos?
I kay pa-GAHR eem-PWESS-tohss SO-bray ESS-tohss ahr-TEE-koo-lohss?

173. How much must I pay?

¿Cuánto tengo que pagar?
KWAHN-toh TEN-go kay pa-GAHR?

174. That is all I have.

Eso es todo lo que tengo.
AY-so ess TOH-doh lo kay TEN-go.

175. Please be careful.

Haga el favor de tener cuidado.
AH-gah el fah-VOR day tay-NAYR kwee-DA-doh.

176. Have you finished?

¿Ha terminado usted?
ah tayr-mee-NA-doh oos-TED?

177. I cannot find my baggage.

Se me perdió el equipaje.
say may payr-DYOH el ay-kee-PA-hay.

178. My train leaves in —— minutes.

Mi tren sale en —— minutos.
mee tren SAH-lay en —— mee-NOO-tohss.

Tickets

Los billetes

183. How much is a ticket to ——?

¿Cuánto cuesta un billete a ——?
*KWAHN-toh KWESS-ta oon bee-YAY-tay ah
——?*

184. One-way ticket.

Un billete sencillo.
oon bee-YAY-tay sen-SEE-yo.

185. A round-trip ticket.

Un billete de ida y vuelta.
oon bee-YAY-tay day EE-da ee VWELL-ta.

186. First-class, second-class, third-class.

Primera clase, segunda clase, tercera clase.
pree-MAY-rah KLAH-say, say-GOON-da KLAH-say, tayr-SAY-rah KLAH-say.

187. Can I go by way of ——?

¿Puedo ir vía ——?
PWAY-doh eer VEE-ah ——?

188. How long is it good for?

¿Por cuántos días es bueno?
por KWAHN-tohss DEE-ahss ess BWAY-no?

189. Can I get something to eat on the way?

¿Se puede comer en camino?
say PWAY-day ko-MAYR en ka-MEE-no?

190. How much baggage may I take?

¿Cuántos kilos de equipaje se permiten llevar?
KWAHN-tohss KEE-lohss day ay-kee-PA-hay say payr-MEE-ten yay-VAHR?

191. How much per kilogram for excess?

¿Cuánto por kilo de exceso?
KWAHN-toh por KEE-lo day ex-SAY-so?

192. Is there travel insurance?

¿Hay seguro para viajeros?
I say-GOO-ro PA-rah vyah-HAY-rohss?

Baggage

El equipaje

197. Where is the baggage room?

¿Dónde se factura el equipaje?
DOHN-day say fahk-TOO-rah el ay-kee-PA-hay?

198. I want to leave these bags for a while.

Quiero dejar estas maletas un rato.
KYAY-ro day-HAHR ESS-tahss ma-LAY-tahss oon RRAH-toh.

199. Do I pay now or later?

¿Debo pagar ahora o después?
DAY-bo pa-GAHR ah-O-rah o dess-PWESS?

200. I want to take out my baggage.

Quiero reclamar mi equipaje.
KYAY-ro rray-klah-MAR mee ay-kee-PA-hay.

201. That is mine there.

Aquél es el mío.
ah-KELL ess el MEE-o.

202. Handle this very carefully.

Mucho cuidado con esto.
MOO-cho kwee-DA-doh kohn ESS-toh.

Train

El tren

207. I am going by train to ——.

Voy en tren a ——.
voy en tren ah ——.

208. At what platform is the train for ——?

¿En qué andén está el tren para ——?
en kay ahn-DEN ess-TA el tren PA-rah ——?

209. Put this in the rack.

Ponga esto en la red.
POHN-gah ESS-toh en la rred.

210. Is the train for —— on time?

¿Está a la hora el tren para ——?
ess-TA ah la O-rah el tren PA-rah ——?

211. It is 10 minutes late.

Está retrasado diez minutos.
ess-TA rray-tra-SAH-doh dyess mee-NOO-tohss.

212. Please close (open) the window.

Favor de cerrar (abrir) la ventanilla.
fah-VOR day say-RRAHR (ah-BREER) la ven-ta-NEE-ya.

213. Where is the diner (the smoker)?

¿Dónde está el comedor (el carro fumador)?
DOHN-day ess-TA el ko-may-DOR (el KA-rro foo-mah-DOR)?

214. Do you mind my smoking?

¿Le molesta que fume?
lay mo-LESS-tah kay FOO-may?

215. Can you give me a match?

¿Puede usted darme un fósforo?
PWAY-day oos-TED DAHR-may oon FOSS-fo-ro?

216. What time is breakfast?

¿A qué hora sirven el desayuno?
ah kay O-rah SEER-ven el dess-ah-YOO-no?

Airplane. El avión

221. Is there motor service to the airport?

¿Hay servicio de transporte al aeropuerto?
I sayr-VEE-syo day trahnss-POR-tay ahl ah-ay-ro-PWAYR-toh?

222. At what time will they come for me?

¿A qué hora vienen por mí?
ah kay O-rah VYAY-nen por mee?

223. When is there a plane to ——?

¿A qué hora sale el avión para ——?
ah kay O-rah SAH-lay el ah-VYOHN PA-rah ——?

224. Is food served on the plane?

¿Se sirven comidas en el aeroplano?
say SEER-ven ko-MEE-dahss en el ah-ay-ro-PLAH-no?

225. How much baggage may I take?

¿Cuántos kilos de equipaje puedo llevar?
KWAHN-tohss KEE-lohss day ay-kee-PA-hay PWAY-doh yay-VAHR?

Bus El Autobús

230. How often do the busses go to ——?

¿Con qué frecuencia salen los buses a ——?
kohn kay fray-KWEN-syah SAH-len lohss BOO-sess ah ——?

231. Can I buy an excursion ticket?

¿Puedo comprar un billete de excursión?
*PWAY-doh kohm-PRAHR oon bee-YAY-tay day
ex-koor-SYOHN?*

232. Is there a stop for lunch?

¿Paran para comer?
PA-rahn PA-rah ko-MAYR?

233. Can one stop over on the way?

¿Se puede hacer escalas en el camino?
*say PWAY-day ah-SAYR ess-KA-lahss en el
ka-MEE-no?*

Boat El barco

238. Can one go by boat to ——?

¿Se puede ir por vapor a ——?
say PWAY-day eer por vah-POR ah ——?

239. When does the next boat leave?

¿Cuándo sale el próximo barco?
*KWAHN-doh SAH-lay el PROHK-see-mo BÁR-
ko?*

240. When must I go on board?

¿A qué hora debo embarcarme?
ah kay O-rah DAY-bo em-bar-KAR-may?

241. Can I land at ——?

¿Puedo desembarcar en ——?
PWAY-doh dess-em-bar-KAR en ——?

242. Are meals served on the boat?

¿Se sirven comidas a bordo?
say SEER-ven ko-MEE-dahss ah BOR-doh?

243. The captain, the purser.

El capitán, el contador.
el ka-pee-TAHN, el kohn-ta-DOR.

244. The steward, on deck.

El camarero, sobre cubierta.
el ka-ma-RAY-ro, SO-bray koo-BYAYR-ta.

245. I want to rent a deck chair.

Quiero alquilar una silla.
KYAY-ro ahl-kee-LAHR OO-na SEE-yah.

246. I am a little seasick.

Estoy un poco mareado.
ess-TOY oon PO-ko ma-ray-AH-doh.

247. I am going to my cabin.

Voy a mi camarote.
voy ah mee ka-ma-RO-tay.

248. Let's go to the dining salon (the bar).

Vamos al comedor (al bar *or* a la cantina).
VAH-mohss ahl ko-may-DOR (ahl bar or ah la kahn-TEE-na).

249. A lifeboat, a life preserver.

Una lancha, un salvavidas.
OO-na LAHN-cha, oon sahl-vah-VEE-dahss.

AUTOMOBILE
Motoring

EL AUTOMÓVIL
En auto

255. Where is there a gas station (a garage)?

¿Dónde hay un expendio de gasolina (un garaje)?

DOHN-day I oon ex-PEN-dyo day gah-so-LEE-na (oon gah-RAH-hay)?

256. Can you recommend a mechanic?

¿Quiere usted recomendarme un mecánico?

KYAY-ray oos-TED rray-ko-men-DAHR-may oon may-KA-nee-ko?

257. I have an international driver's license.

Tengo una licencia automovilista internacional.

TEN-go OO-na lee-SEN-syah out-o-mo-vee-LEESS-ta een-tayr-na-syo-NAHL.

258. Is it hard surface or dirt?

¿Está pavimentado o es de tierra?

ess-TA pa-vee-men-TA-doh o ess day TYAY-rrah?

259. What is this (the next) town?

¿Cómo se llama este (el próximo) pueblo?

KO-mo say YAH-ma ESS-tay (el PROHK-see-mo) PWAY-blo?

260. Where does that road go?

¿Adónde conduce aquel camino?

ah-DOHN-day kohn-DOO-say ah-KELL ka-MEE-no?

261. Where is the auto club?

¿Dónde está la asociación automovilística?
DOHN-day ess-TA la ah-so-syah-SYOHN out-o-mo-vee-LEESS-tee-ka?

262. I want some air.

Quiero aire.
KYAY-ro I-ray.

263. How much is gas a liter?

¿Cuánto cuesta la gasolina por litro?
KWAHN-to KWESS-ta la gah-so-LEE-na por LEE-tro?

264. Give me —— liters of gasoline.

Déme —— litros de gasolina.
DAY-may —— LEE-trohss day gah-so-LEE-na.

265. Please change the oil.

Por favor, cambie el aceite.
por fah-VOR, KAHM-byay el ah-SAY-tay.

266. Light (medium, heavy) oil.

Aceite delgado (mediano, grueso).
ah-SAY-tay del-GAH-doh (may-DYAH-no, GRWAY-so).

267. Put water in the battery.

Ponga agua en el acumulador.
POHN-gah AH-gwa en el ah-koo-moo-la-DOR.

268. Will you lubricate the car?

¿Quiere engrasar el coche?
KYAY-ray en-grah-SAHR el KO-chay?

269. Could you wash it now (soon)?

¿Podría lavarlo ahora (pronto)?
po-DREE-ah la-VAHR-lo ah-O-rah (PROHN-toh)?

270. Tighten the brakes.

Ajuste los frenos.
ah-HOOSS-tay lohss FRAY-nohss.

271. Will you check the tires?

¿Quiere usted revisar los neumáticos *or* las llantas?
KYAY-ray oos-TED rray-vee-SAHR lohss nay-oo-MA-tee-kohss or lahss YAHN-tahss?

272. Change this tire (wheel).

Cambie este neumático (esta rueda).
KAHM-byay ESS-tay nay-oo-MA-tee-ko (ESS-ta RRWAY-da).

273. A puncture, a slow leak.

Un pinchazo, un escape.
oon peen-CHA-so, oon ess-KAH-pay.

274. The —— does not work (well).

——no funciona (bien).
——no foon-SYO-na (byen).

275. What is wrong?

¿Qué tiene?
kay TYAY-nay?

276. The engine overheats.

El motor se calienta.
el mo-TOHR say ka-LYEN-ta.

277. It skips (stalls).

El motor falla (se para).
el mo-TOHR FAH-yah (say PA-rah).

278. There is a grinding (a leak, a noise).

Hay un rechinamiento (un goteo, un ruido).
I oon rray-chee-na-MYEN-toh (oon go-TAY-o, oon RRWEE-doh).

279. There is a rattle (a squeak) in ——.

Hay un golpeteo (un chirrido) en ——.
I oon gohl-pay-TAY-o (oon chee-RREE-doh) en ——.

280. May I park here for a while?

¿Me permite estacionarme aquí un rato?
may payr-MEE-tay ess-ta-syo-NAHR-may ah-KEE oon RRAH-toh?

281. I want to garage my car for the night.

Quiero guardar mi auto por la noche.
KYAY-ro gwahr-DAHR mee OUT-o por la NO-chay.

282. What time does it close (open)?

¿A qué hora se cierra (se abre)?
ah kay O-rah say SYAY-rrah (say AH-bray)?

Help on the Road   La ayuda en el camino

287. My car has broken down.

Mi coche no funciona.
mee KO-chay no foon-SYO-na.

288. I am sorry to trouble you.

Siento mucho incomodarle.
SYEN-toh MOO-cho een-ko-mo-DAHR-lay.

289. Can you tow (push) me?

¿Puede usted remolcarme (empujarme)?
PWAY-day oos-TED rray-mohl-KAR-may (em-poo-HAHR-may)?

290. Can you help me jack up the car?

¿Puede usted ayudarme a alzar el carro con el gato?
PWAY-day oos-TED ah-yoo-DAHR-may ah ahl-SAHR el KAH-rro kohn el GAH-toh?

291. Will you put on the spare?

¿Quiere usted poner la rueda de repuesto?
KYAY-ray oos-TED po-NAYR la RRWAY-da day rray-PWESS-toh?

292. Could you give me some (gas)?

¿Puede usted darme un poco (de gasolina)?
PWAY-day oos-TED DAHR-may oon PO-ko (day gah-so-LEE-na)?

293. Will you take me to a garage?

¿Quiere usted llevarme a un garaje?
KYAY-ray oos-TED yay-VAHR-may ah oon gah-RAH-hay?

294. It is in the ditch.

Está en la zanja.
ess-TA en la SAHN-ha.

295. Will you help get the car off the road?
¿Quiere usted ayudarme a apartar el coche del camino?
KYAY-ray oos-TED ah-yoo-DAHR-may ah ah-par-TAR el KO-chay del ka-MEE-no?

296. My car is stuck in the mud.
Mi carro está atascado.
mee KAH-rro ess-TA ah-tahss-KA-doh.

Parts of the Car   Las partes del carro

301. Accelerator.   El acelerador.
el ah-say-lay-rah-DOR.

302. Battery.   El acumulador.
el ah-koo-moo-la-DOR.

303. Bolt.   El tornillo.   *el tor-NEE-yo.*

304. Brake.   El freno.   *el FRAY-no.*

305. Engine.   El motor.   *el mo-TOHR.*

306. Lights.   Las luces.   *lahss LOO-sess.*

307. Spring.   El muelle.   *el MWAY-yay.*

308. Starter.   El arranque.   *el ah-RRAHN-kay.*

309. Steering wheel.   El volante.
el vo-LAHN-tay.

310. Tail light.   El foco trasero.
el FO-ko tra-SAY-ro.

311. Tire.   La llanta *or* el neumático.
la YAHN-ta or el nay-oo-MA-tee-ko.

312. Spare wheel.   Rueda de repuesto.
RRWAY-da day rray-PWESS-toh.

313. Tube (inner). La cámara *or* el tubo.
la KA-ma-rah or *el TOO-bo.*

314. Wheel (back). La rueda (trasera).
la RRWAY-da (tra-SAY-rah).

315. Front. Delantera. *day-lahn-TAY-rah.*

316. Left. De la izquierda. *day la eess-KYAYR-da.*

317. Right. De la derecha. *day la day-RAY-cha.*

Tools and Equipment

Las herramientas y el equipo

322. Chains. Las cadenas. *lahss ka-DAY-nahss.*

323. Hammer. El martillo. *el mar-TEE-yo.*

324. Jack. El gato. *el GAH-toh.*

325. Key. La llave. *la YAH-vay.*

326. Pliers. Las pinzas. *lahss PEEN-sahss.*

327. Rope. Una soga. *OO-na SO-gah.*

328. Screwdriver. El desatornillador.
el dess-ah-tor-nee-yah-DOR.

329. Tire pump. La bomba de neumáticos.
la BOHM-ba day nay-oo-MA-tee-kohss.

330. Monkey wrench. La llave inglesa.
la YAH-vay een-GLAY-sah.

Road Signs, Public Notices

Los letreros del camino, etc.

*This section has been alphabetized in Spanish to facilitate
the tourist's reading of Spanish signs.*

335. Go. Adelante. *ah-day-LAHN-tay.*

336. Stop. Alto. *AHL-toh.*

337. Avenue. Avenida. *ah-vay-NEE-da.*

338. Steep Grade. Bajada. *ba-HA-da.*

339. Boulevard. Bulevar. *boo-lay-VAHR.*

340. High Tension Lines.
Cables de alta tensión.
KAH-bless day AHL-ta ten-SYOHN.

341. Narrow Road. Camino angosto.
ka-MEE-no ahn-GOHSS-toh.

342. Road Repairs. Camino en reparación.
ka-MEE-no en rray-pa-rah-SYOHN.

343. Road Intersection. Camino lateral.
ka-MEE-no la-tay-RAHL.

344. Winding Road. Camino sinuoso.
ka-MEE-no see-NWO-so.

345. Closed. Cerrado. *say-RRAH-doh.*

346. Sharp Turn. Codo. *KO-doh.*

347. Dip. Columpio. *ko-LOOM-pyo.*

348. Keep Right. Conserve su derecha.
kohn-SAYR-vay soo day-RAY-cha.

349. Crossroads. Cruce. *KROO-say.*

350. Curve. Curva. *KOOR-vah.*

351. Double (Reverse) Curve.
Curva doble (inversa).
KOOR-vah DOH-blay (een-VAYR-sah).

352. Dangerous Curve. Curva peligrosa.
KOOR-vah pay-lee-GRO-sah.

353. Dip. Depresión. *day-pray-SYOHN.*

354. Slow. Despacio. *dess-PA-syo.*

355. Detour. Desvío. *dess-VEE-o.*

356. Junction. Empalme. *em-PAHL-may.*

357. Entrance. Entrada. *en-TRA-da.*

358. School. Escuela. *ess-KWAY-la.*

359. Parking. Estacionamiento.
ess-ta-syo-na-MYEN-toh.

360. Railroad Crossing. F. C. (Ferrocarril).
(*fay-rro-ka-RREEL*).

361. Pavement Ends. Fin del pavimento.
feen del pa-vee-MEN-toh.

362. Slow Down. Modere su velocidad.
mo-DAY-ray soo vay-lo-see-DAHD.

363. No Thoroughfare. No hay paso. *no I PA-so.*

364. Full Stop. Parada obligatoria.
pa-RAH-da o-blee-gah-TOH-ryah.

365. Stop, Look and Listen.
Pare, mire y escuche.
PA-ray, MEE-ray ee ess-KOO-chay.

366. Danger. Precaución. *pray-cow-SYOHN.*

367. No Right (Left) Turn.
Prohibida vuelta a la derecha (izquierda).
*pro-ee-BEE-da VWELL-ta ah la day-RAY-cha
(eess-KYAYR-da).*

368. Keep Out. Prohibido el paso.
pro-ee-BEE-doh el PA-so.

369. No Parking. Prohibido estacionarse.
pro-ee-BEE-doh ess-ta-syo-NAHR-say.

370. Narrow Bridge. Puente angosto.
PWEN-tay ahn-GOHSS-toh.

371. Temporary Bridge. Puente provisional.
PWEN-tay pro-vee-syo-NAHL.

372. Exit. Salida. *sah-LEE-da.*

373. One-way. Sentido único.
sen-TEE-doh OO-nee-ko.

374. Maximum Speed. Velocidad máxima.
vay-lo-see-DAHD MAHK-see-ma.

375. Kilometers Per Hour. Km. por hora.
kee-LO-may-trohss por O-rah.

376. No smoking. Se prohibe fumar.
say pro-EE-bay foo-MAR.

377. Men. Caballeros *or* Señores.
ka-ba-YAY-rohss or say-NYO-ress.

378. Ladies. Damas *or* Señoras *or* Mujeres.
DA-mahss or say-NYO-rahss or moo-HAY-ress.

Streetcar and Local Bus

El tranvía y el autobús

382. The bus stop.
La parada.
la pa-RAH-da.

383. The conductor, driver.
El conductor, el chofer.
el kohn-dook-TOR, el cho-FAYR.

384. What bus (streetcar) do I take for ——?
¿Qué autobús (tranvía) tomo para ——?
kay out-o-BOOSS (trahn-VEE-ah) TOH-mo PA-rah ——?

385. Where does the bus for —— stop?
¿Dónde para el bus para ——?
DOHN-day PA-rah el booss PA-rah ——?

386. Do you go near ——?
¿Pasa usted cerca de ——?
PA-sa oos-TED SAYR-ka day ——?

387. How much is the fare?
¿Cuánto cuesta el pasaje?
KWAHN-toh KWESS-ta el pa-SAH-hay?

388. A transfer, please.
Un transbordo, por favor.
oon trahnss-BOR-doh, por fah-VOR.

389. The next stop.
La próxima parada.
la PROHK-see-ma pa-RAH-da.

390. Two blocks more.
Dos cuadras más.
dohss KWAH-drahss mahss.

Taxi   El taxi

395. Please call me a taxi.
Haga el favor de llamarme un taxi.
AH-gah el fah-VOR day yah-MAR-may oon TAHK-see.

396. How far is it?
¿A qué distancia está?
ah kay deess-TAHN-syah ess-TA?

397. How much will it cost?
¿Cuánto costará?
KWAHN-toh koss-ta-RAH?

398. That is too much.
Eso es demasiado.
Ay-so ess day-mah-SYAH-doh.

401. Please drive slower.
Por favor, conduzca más despacio.
por fah-VOR, kohn-DOOSS-ka mahss dess-PA-syo.

402. Drive more carefully.
Maneje con más cuidado.
ma-NAY-hay kohn mahss kwee-DA-doh.

403. Stop here. Wait for me.
Pare aquí. Espéreme.
PA-ray ah-KEE. ess-PAY-ray-may.

404. Go by way of ——.
Vaya por ——.
VAH-yah por - ——.

405. How much do I owe you?
¿Cuánto le debo?
KWAHN-toh lay DAY-bo?

LODGING. EL ALOJAMIENTO

The Hotel and Inn El hotel y la posada

410. Which hotel is good (inexpensive)?
¿Qué hotel es bueno (barato)?
kay o-TEL ess BWAY-no (ba-RAH-toh)?

411. The best hotel.
El mejor hotel.
el may-HOR o-TEL.

412. Not too expensive.
No muy caro.
no mwee KAH-ro.

413. I (don't) want to be in the center of town.
(No) quiero estar en el centro.
(no) KYAY-ro ess-TAR en el SEN-tro.

414. Where it is not noisy.
Donde no haya ruido.
DOHN-day no AH-yah RRWEE-doh.

415. I have a reservation for ——.
Tengo reservado ——.
TEN-go rray-sayr-VAH-doh ——.

416. I want to make a reservation for ——.
Quiero reservar ——.
KYAY-ro rray-sayr-VAHR ——.

417. I want a room with (without) meals.
Quiero un cuarto con (sin) comidas.
KYAY-ro oon KWAHR-toh kohn (seen) ko-MEE-dahss.

418. I want a single (double) room.
Quiero un cuarto para uno (para dos).
KYAY-ro oon KWAHR-toh PA-rah OO-no (PA-rah dohss).

419. A suite.
Una suite.
OO-na SWEE-tay.

420. With bath, shower, twin beds.
Con baño, ducha, camas gemelas.
kohn BA-nyo, DOO-cha, KA-mahss hay-MAY-lahss.

421. A room with a window.
Un cuarto con ventana.
oon KWAHR-toh kohn ven-TA-na.

422. In the front, at the back.
Al frente, al fondo.
ahl FREN-tay, ahl FOHN-doh.

423. For a few (two) days.
Por unos (dos) días.
por OO-nohss (dohss) DEE-ahss.

424. For tonight.
Por esta noche.
por ESS-ta NO-chay.

425. For —— persons.
Para —— personas.
PA-rah —— payr-SO-nahss.

426. What is the rate a day?
¿Cuánto cuesta por día?
KWAHN-toh KWESS-ta por DEE-ah?

427. A week, a month.
Por semana, por mes.
por say-MA-na, por mess.

428. On what floor?
¿En qué piso?
en kay PEE-so?

429. Is there an elevator?
¿Hay ascensor?
I ahss-sen-SOR?

430. Running water, hot water.
Agua corriente, agua caliente.
AH-gwa ko-RRYEN-tay, AH-gwa ka-LYEN-tay.

431. Up (stairs), down (stairs).

Arriba, abajo.
ah-RREE-ba, ah-BA-ho.

432. I want a room higher up.

Quiero un cuarto en un piso más alto.
KYAY-ro oon KWAHR-toh en oon PEE-so mahss
AHL-toh.

433. On a lower floor.

En un piso más bajo.
en oon PEE-so mahss BA-ho.

434. I should like to see the room.

Quisiera ver el cuarto.
kee-SYAY-rah vayr el KWAHR-toh.

435. Where is the bathroom?

¿Dónde está el baño?
DOHN-day ess-TA el BA-nyo?

436. I (do not) like this one.

Éste (no) me gusta.
ESS-tay (no) may GOOSS-ta.

437. Have you something better?

¿Tiene usted uno mejor?
TYAY-nay oos-TED OO-no may-HOR?

438. Cheaper, larger, something smaller.

Más barato, más grande, algo más pequeño.
mahss ba-RAH-toh, mahss GRAHN-day, AHL-go
mahss pay-KAY-nyo.

439. With more light (air).

Con más luz (más ventilación).
kohn mahss looss (mahss ven-tee-la-SYOHN).

440. I have baggage at the station.

Tengo equipaje en la estación.
TEN-go ay-kee-PA-hay en la ess-ta-SYOHN.

441. Send me a bellboy.

Mándeme un botones.
MAHN-day-may oon bo-TOH-ness.

442. Will you send for my bags?

¿Quiere usted mandar por mis maletas?
KYAY-ray oos-TED mahn-DAR por meess ma-LAY-tahss?

443. Here is the check for my trunk.

Aquí tiene usted el talón de mi baúl.
ah-KEE TYAY-nay oos-TED el ta-LOHN day mee ba-OOL.

444. Please send —— to my room.

Haga el favor de mandar —— a mi cuarto.
AH-gah el fah-VOR day mahn-DAHR —— ah mee KWAHR-toh.

445. Ice, ice water.

Hielo, agua helada.
YAY-lo, AH-gwa ay-LA-da.

446. Please call me at —— o'clock.

Haga el favor de llamarme a ——.
AH-gah el fah-VOR day yah-MAR-may ah ——.

447. I want breakfast in my room.

Quiero el desayuno en mi cuarto.
KYAY-ro el dess-ah-YOO-no en mee KWAHR-toh.

448. Please get me ——.

Haga el favor de conseguirme ——.
AH-gah el fah-VOR day kohn-say-GEAR-may
——.

449. Could I have some laundry done?

¿Me pueden lavar la ropa?
may PWAY-den la-VAHR la RRO-pa?

450. I want some things pressed.

Quiero hacer planchar unos vestidos.
KYAY-ro ah-SAYR plahn-CHAR OO-nohss vess-
TEE-dohss.

451. My room key, please.

Mi llave, por favor.
mee YAH-vay, por fah-VOR.

452. Have I letters or messages?

¿Hay cartas o mensajes para mí?
I KAR-tahss o men-SAH-hess PA-rah mee?

453. When does the mail come?

¿A qué hora llega el correo?
ah kay O-rah YAY-gah el ko-RRAY-o?

454. What is my room number?

¿Cuál es el número de mi cuarto?
kwahl ess el NOO-may-ro day mee KWAHR-toh?

455. I am leaving at —— o'clock.

Salgo a ——.
SAHL-go ah ——.

456. Please make out my bill.

Favor de preparar mi cuenta.
fah-VOR day pray-pa-RAHR mee KWEN-ta.

457. I should like to speak to the manager.

Quisiera hablar con el gerente.
kee-SYAY-rah ah-BLAHR kohn el hay-REN-tay.

458. Can one store baggage here until ——?

¿Se puede guardar aquí el equipaje hasta
——?
say PWAY-day gwahr-DAHR ah-KEE el ay-kee-PA-hay AHSS-ta ——?

459. Forward my mail to ——.

Reexpídame las cartas a ——.
rray-ex-PEE-da-may lahss KAR-tahss ah ——.

Chambermaid   La camarera

464. Do not disturb me until ——.

No me moleste hasta ——.
no may mo-LESS-tay AHSS-ta —— -.

465. Please change the sheets today.

Favor de cambiar hoy las sábanas.
fah-VOR day kahm-BYAHR oy lahss SAH-ba-nahss.

466. Bring me another pillow (blanket).

Tráigame otra almohada (frazada).
TRY-gah-may O-tra ahl-mo-AH-da (frah-SAH-da).

467. A pillow case, bath mat.

Una funda, un tapete de baño.
OO-na FOON-da, oon ta-PAY-tay day BA-nyo.

468. More hangers, a glass.

Más ganchos, un vaso.
mahss GAHN-chohss, oon VAH-so.

469. Soap, towels, a candle.

Jabón, toallas, una vela.
ha-BOHN, toh-AH-yahss, OO-na VAY-la.

470. Drinking water, toilet paper.

Agua para beber, papel higiénico.
AH-gwa PA-rah bay-BAYR, pa-PELL ee-HYAY-nee-ko.

471. Is there always hot water?

¿Siempre hay agua caliente?
SYEM-pray I AH-gwa ka-LYEN-tay?

472. Please spray for mosquitoes.

Por favor, use el Flit.
por fah-VOR, OO-say el fleet.

473. Please come back later.

Favor de volver más tarde.
fah-VOR day vohl-VAYR mahss TAR-day.

Apartment   El apartamiento

478. I want a furnished apartment.

Quiero un apartamiento amueblado.
KYAY-ro oon ah-par-ta-MYEN-toh ah-mway-BLA-doh.

479. I want a living room, —— bedrooms.

Quiero una sala, —— alcobas.
KYAY-ro OO-na SAH-la, —— ahl-KO-bahss.

480. A dining room, a kitchen.

Un comedor, una cocina.
oon ko-may-DOR, OO-na ko-SEE-na.

481. A patio, a private bath.

Un patio, un baño particular.
oon PA-tyo, oon BA-nyo par-tee-koo-LAHR.

482. Is the linen furnished?

¿Eso incluye sábanas y mantelería?
AY-so een-KLOO-yay SAH-ba-nahss ee mahn-tay-lay-REE-ah?

483. How much is it a month?

¿Cuánto es por mes?
KWAHN-toh ess por mess?

484. The blankets, silver and dishes.

Las frazadas, la vajilla.
lahss frah-SAH-dahss, la vah-HEE-yah.

485. Can I get a maid?

¿Puedo conseguir una criada?
PWAY-doh kohn-say-GEAR OO-na kree-AH-da?

486. Do you know a good cook?

¿Conoce usted a una buena cocinera?
ko-NO-say oos-TED ah OO-na BWAY-na ko-see-NAY-rah?

487. Where can I rent a garage?

¿Dónde puedo alquilar un garaje?
DOHN-day PWAY-doh ahl-kee-LAHR oon gah-RAH-hay?

488. We will return at 12:30.

Volvemos a las doce y media.
vohl-VAY-mohss ah lahss DOH-say ee MAY-dyah.

RESTAURANT

EL RESTAURANTE

492. Where is there a good restaurant?

¿Dónde hay un buen restaurante?
DOHN-day I oon bwen rress-ta-oo-RAHN-tay?

493. For breakfast, lunch.

Para el desayuno, el almuerzo.
PA-rah el dess-ah-YOO-no, el ahl-MWAYR-so.

494. Dinner, a sandwich.

La comida, un sandwich.
la ko-MEE-da, oon sandwich.

495. Between what hours is dinner served?

¿Entre qué horas se sirve la comida?
EN-tray kay O-rahss say SEER-vay la ko-MEE-da?

496. Can we lunch (dine) now?

¿Podemos almorzar (comer) ahora?
po-DAY-mohss ahl-mor-SAHR (ko-MAYR) ah-O-rah?

497. There are two (five) of us.

Somos dos (cinco).
SO-mohss dohss (SEEN-ko).

498. The head waiter, waiter, waitress.

El jefe de camareros, el camarero, la camarera.
el HAY-fay day ka-ma-RAY-rohss, el ka-ma-RAY-ro, la ka-ma-RAY-rah.

499. Give me a table near the window.

Déme una mesa cerca de la ventana.
DAY-may OO-na MAY-sah SAYR-ka day la ven-TA-na.

500. At the side, in the corner.

Al lado, en el rincón.
ahl LA-doh, en el rreen-KOHN.

501. Waiter !

¡ Mozo! *or* ¡ Camarero!
MO-so! or *ka-ma-RAY-ro!*

502. Is this table reserved?

¿ Está reservada esta mesa?
ess-TA rray-sayr-VAH-da ESS-ta MAY-sah?

503. We want to dine à la carte.

Deseamos comer a la carta.
day-say-AH-mohss ko-MAYR ah la KAR-ta.

504. Please serve us quickly.

Haga el favor de servirnos de prisa.
*AH-gah el fah-VOR day sayr-VEER-nohss day
    PREE-sah.*

505. Bring me the menu.

Tráigame la carta.
TRY-gah-may la KAR-ta.

506. The wine list.

La carta de vinos.
la KAR-ta day VEE-nohss.

507. I want something simple.

Quiero algo sencillo.
KYAY-ro AHL-go sen-SEE-yo.

508. Not too spicy.

No muy picante.
no mwee pee-KAHN-tay.

509. A napkin, a glass.

Una servilleta, un vaso.
OO-na sayr-vee-YAY-ta, oon VAH-so.

510. A plate, a knife.

Un plato, un cuchillo.
oon PLAH-toh, oon koo-CHEE-yo.

511. A fork, a large spoon.

Un tenedor, una cuchara.
oon tay-nay-DOR, OO-na koo-CHA-rah.

512. A teaspoon.

Una cucharita.
OO-na koo-cha-REE-ta.

513. The bread, the butter.

El pan, la mantequilla.
el pahn, la mahn-tay-KEE-yah.

514. The cream, the sugar.

La crema, el azúcar.
la KRAY-ma, el ah-SOO-kar.

515. The salt, pepper.

La sal, la pimienta.
la sahl, la pee-MYEN-ta.

516. The sauce, the vinegar, the (salad) oil.

La salsa, el vinagre, el aceite.
la SAHL-sah, el vee-NA-gray, el ah-SAY-tay.

517. I have had enough, thanks.

Basta, gracias.
BAHSS-ta, GRAH-syahss.

518. This is not clean.

> Esto no está limpio.
> *ESS-toh no ess-TA LEEM-pyo.*

519. It is dirty.

> Está sucio.
> *ess-TA SOO-syo.*

520. A little more of this.

> Un poco más de esto.
> *oon PO-ko mahss day ESS-toh.*

521. I like it rare (well done).

> Me gusta bien cruda (bien cocida).
> *may GOOSS-ta byen KROO-da (byen ko-SEE-da).*

522. This is over-cooked.

> Esto está demasiado cocido.
> *ESS-toh ess-TA day-ma-SYAH-doh ko-SEE-doh.*

523. That is not cooked enough.

> Eso no está bastante cocido.
> *AY-so no ess-TA bahss-TAHN-tay ko-SEE-doh.*

524. This is too tough (sweet, sour).

> Esto está muy duro (dulce, agrio).
> *ESS-toh ess-TA mwee DOO-ro (DOOL-say, AH-gree-o).*

525. This is cold.

> Esto está frío.
> *ESS-toh ess-TA FREE-o.*

526. Take it away.

Lléveselo.
YAY-vay-say-lo.

527. I did not order this.

No he pedido esto.
no ay pay-DEE-doh ESS-toh.

528. May I change this for (fruit)?

¿Se puede cambiar esto por (fruta)?
say PWAY-day kahm-BYAHR ESS-toh por (FROO-ta)?

529. Ask the headwaiter to come here.

Pida al jefe que venga acá.
PEE-da ahl HAY-fay kay VEN-gah ah-KA.

530. The check, please.

La cuenta, por favor.
la KWEN-ta, por fah-VOR.

531. Kindly pay at the cashier's.

Haga el favor de pagar en la caja.
AH-gah el fa-VOR day pa-GAHR en la KAH-ha.

532. Keep the change for yourself.

El cambio es para usted.
el KAHM-byo ess PA-rah oos-TED.

533. There is a mistake in the bill.

Hay un error en la cuenta.
I oon ay-RROR en la KWEN-ta.

534. What are these charges for?

¿Qué son estas extras?
kay sohn ESS-tahss EX-trahss?

535. Is the tip included?
¿Está incluída la propina?
ess-TA een-KLWEE-da la pro-PEE-na?

536. Is there a service charge?
¿Hay que pagar por el servicio?
I kay pa-GAHR por el sayr-VEE-syo?

Café. El café

541. Bartender. Cantinero. *kahn-tee-NAY-ro.*

542. Waiter. Mozo. *MO-so.*

543. A cocktail. Un cocktail. *oon cock-tail.*

544. A fruit drink. Una bebida.
OO-na bay-BEE-da.

545. A highball. Un highball. *oon highball.*

546. Ice water. Agua helada. *AH-gwa ay-LA-da.*

547. A liqueur. Un licor. *oon lee-KOHR.*

548. Brandy. Aguardiente. *ah-gwahr-DYEN-tay.*

549. Light (dark) beer. Cerveza clara (oscura).
sayr-VAY-sah KLAH-rah (ohss-KOO-rah).

551. White (red) wine. Vino blanco (tinto).
VEE-no BLAHN-ko (TEEN-toh).

552. A soft drink. Un refresco.
oon rray-FRESS-ko.

553. A bottle of ——. Una botella de ——.
OO-na bo-TAY-yah day ——.

554. A glass of–. Un vaso de–. *oon VAH-so day —.*

555. Let's have another. Tomemos otro más.
toh-MAY-mohss O-tro mahss.

FOOD LOS ALIMENTOS *

*This section has been alphabetized in Spanish to facilitate
the tourist's reading of Spanish menus.*

560. Olives. Aceitunas. *ah-say-TOO-nahss.*

561. Biscuit. Bizcocho. *bees-KO-cho.*

562. Sweet roll. Bollo. *BO-yo.*

563. Tuna. Bonito. *bo-NEE-toh.*

564. Pudding. Budín. *boo-DEEN.*

565. Doughnut *or* **fritter.** Buñuelo.
boo-NWAY-lo.

566. Peanuts. Cacahuates. *ka-ka-WAH-tess.*

567. Coffee (with milk, cream).
Café (con leche, con crema).
ka-FAY (kohn LAY-chay, kohn KRAY-ma).

568. Black coffee. Café solo. *ka-FAY SO-lo.*

569. Pumpkin *or* **squash.** Calabaza.
ka-la-BA-sah.

570. (Chicken) broth. Caldo (de pollo).
KAHL-doh (day PO-yo).

571. Shrimps. Camarones. *ka-ma-RO-ness.*

572. Sweet potato. Camote. *ka-MO-tay.*

573. Crab. Cangrejo. *kahn-GRAY-ho.*

574. Meat. Carne. *KAR-nay.*

575. (Roast, broiled) beef.
Carne de vaca (asada, a la parrilla).
*KAR-nay day VAH-ka (ah-SAH-da, ah la pa-
RREE-yah).*

576. Mutton. Carnero. *kar-NAY-ro.*

577. Onion. Cebolla. *say-BO-yah.*

*An extensive list of Spanish food can be found on pages
117-28.

578. Cherry. Cereza. *say-RAY-sah.*

579. Sausage. Chorizo. *cho-REE-so.*

580. Chop. Chuleta. *choo-LAY-ta.*

581. Stew. Cocido. *ko-SEE-doh.*

582. Cabbage. Col. *kohl.*

583. Cauliflower. Coliflor. *ko-lee-FLOHR.*

584. Stewed fruit. Compota. *kohm-PO-ta.*

585. Rabbit. Conejo. *ko-NAY-ho.*

586. Jam. Conserva. *kohn-SAYR-vah.*

587. Peach. Durazno. *doo-RAHSS-no.*

588. Meat pie. Empanada. *em-pa-NA-da.*

589. Corncake with meat. Enchilada.
en-chee-LA-da.

590. Pickles. Encurtidos. *en-koor-TEE-dohss.*

591. Salad. Ensalada. *en-sah-LA-da.*

592. Hors d'oeuvre. Entremeses.
en-tray-MAY-sess.

593. Pickled fish. Escabeche. *ess-ka-BAY-chay.*

594. Asparagus. Espárragos. *ess-PA-rrah-gohss.*

595. Spinach. Espinacas. *ess-pee-NA-kahss.*

596. Meat stew. Estofado. *ess-toh-FAH-doh.*

597. Pheasant. Faisán. *fy-SAHN.*

598. Cold cuts. Fiambres. *FYAHM-bress.*

599. Noodles. Fideos. *fee-DAY-ohss.*

600. Tenderloin. Filete. *fee-LAY-tay.*

601. Custard. Flan. *flahn.*

602. Raspberry. Frambuesa. *frahm-BWAY-sah.*

603. Strawberry. Fresa. *FRAY-sah.*

604. Beans. Frijoles. *free-HO-less.*

605. Chick peas. Garbanzos. *gahr-BAHN-sohss.*

606. Turkey. Guajolote. *gwa-ho-LO-tay.*

607. Stew. Guisado. *ghee-SAH-doh.*

608. Peas. Guisantes. *ghee-SAHN-tess.*

609. Guava. Guayaba. *gwa-YAH-ba.*

610. String beans. Habichuelas.
ah-bee-CHWAY-lahss.

611. Ice cream. Helado. *ay-LA-doh.*

612. Ice cubes. Hielo. *YAY-lo.*

613. Liver. Hígado. *EE-gah-doh.*

614. Fig. Higo. *EE-go.*

615. Mushrooms. Hongos. *OHN-gohss.*

616. Eggs (fried with chile sauce).
Huevos (a la ranchera).
WAY-vohss (ah la rrahn-CHAY-rah).

617. Eggs (hard-boiled). Huevos (duros).
WAY-vohss (DOO-rohss).

618. Eggs (poached). Huevos (escalfados).
WAY-vohss (ess-kahl-FAH-dohss).

619. Eggs (fried). Huevos (fritos).
WAY-vohss (FREE-tohss).

620. Eggs (scrambled). Huevos (revueltos).
WAY-vohss (rray-VWELL-tohss).

621. Jelly. Jalea. *ha-LAY-ah.*

622. Ham. Jamón. *ha-MOHN.*

623. Sherry. Jerez. *hay-RESS.*

624. Hash. Jigote. *hee-GO-tay.*

625. Lobster. Langosta. *lahn-GOHSS-ta.*

626. Milk (condensed, malted).
Leche (condensada, malteada).
LAY-chay (kohn-den-SAH-da, mahl-tay-AH-da).

627. Lettuce. Lechuga. *lay-CHOO-gah.*

628. Vegetables. Legumbres. *lay-GOOM-bress.*

629. Flounder. Lenguado. *len-GWAH-doh.*

630. Lentils. Lentejas. *len-TAY-hahss.*

631. Hare. Liebre. *LYAY-bray.*

632. Lemon. Limón. *lee-MOHN.*

633. Lemonade. Limonada. *lee-mo-NA-da.*

634. Corn. Maíz. *ma-EESS.*

635. Apple. Manzana. *mahn-SAH-na.*

636. Almond paste. Mazapán. *ma-sah-PAHN.*

637. Peach. Melocotón. *may-lo-ko-TOHN.*

638. Melon. Melón. *may-LOHN.*

639. Vegetable soup. Menestra. *may-NESS-tra.*

640. Marmalade. Mermelada. *mayr-may-LA-da.*

641. Bologna. Mortadela. *mohr-ta-DAY-la.*

642. Mustard. Mostaza. *mohss-TA-sah.*

643. Turnip. Nabo. *NA-bo.*

644. Orange. Naranja. *na-RAHN-ha.*

645. Orangeade. Naranjada. *na-rahn-HA-da.*

646. Spanish custard. Natilla. *na-TEE-yah.*

647. Nuts. Nueces. *NWAY-sess.*

648. Yam. Ñame. *NYAH-may.*

649. Oysters. Ostras *or* ostiones. *OHSS-trahss* or *ohss-TYO-ness.*

650. Rolls. Panecillos. *pa-nay-SEE-yohss.*

651. Potatoes. Papas. *PA-pahss.*

652. Raisins. Pasas. *PA-sahss.*

653. Pastry. Pasteles. *pahss-TAY-less.*

654. Potatoes. Patatas. *pa-TA-tahss.*

655. Cucumbers. Pepinos. *pay-PEE-nohss.*

656. Pear. Pera. *PAY-rah.*

657. Perch. Perca. *PAYR-ka.*

658. Partridge. Perdiz. *payr-DEESS.*

659. Parsley. Perejil. *pay-ray-HEEL.*

660. (Fried) fish. Pescado (frito).
pess-KA-doh (FREE-toh).

661. Hash. Picadillo. *pee-ka-DEE-yo.*

662. Peppers. Pimientos. *pee-MYEN-tohss.*

663. Pineapple. Piña. *PEE-nyah.*

664. Bananas. Plátanos. *PLAH-ta-nohss.*

665. Chicken. Pollo. *PO-yo.*

666. Broiled chicken. Pollo a la parrilla.
PO-yo ah la pa-RREE-yah.

667. Dessert. Postre. *POHSS-tray.*

668. Boiled meat with vegetables. Puchero.
poo-CHAY-ro.

669. Pork. Puerco. *PWAYR-ko.*

670. Pudding. Pudín. *poo-DEEN.*

671. Mashed potatoes. Puré de papas.
poo-RAY day PA-pahss.

672. Cheese. Queso. *KAY-so.*

673. Radishes. Rábanos. *RRAH-ba-nohss.*

674. Slice. Rebanada. *rray-ba-NA-da.*

675. Cottage cheese. Requesón.
rray-kay-SOHN.

676. Kidneys. Riñones. *rree-NYO-ness.*

677. Haddock. Robalo. *rro-BA-lo.*

678. Roast Beef. Rosbif. *rrohss-BEEF*.

679. Sausage. Salchicha. *sahl-CHEE-cha*.

680. Salami. Salchichón. *sahl-chee-CHOHN*.

681. Salmon. Salmón. *sahl-MOHN*.

682. Chopped meat. Salpicón. *sahl-pee-KOHN*.

683. Sauce. Salsa. *SAHL-sah*.

684. Watermelon. Sandía. *sahn-DEE-ah*.

685. Sardine. Sardina. *sahr-DEE-na*.

686. Brains. Sesos. *SAY-sohss*.

687. Mushrooms. Setas. *SAY-tahss*.

688. Clear (thick) soup. Sopa clara (espesa). *SO-pa KLAH-rah (ess-PAY-sah)*.

689. Sherbet. Sorbete. *sor-BAY-tay*.

690. Pie or tart. Tarta. *TAR-ta*.

691. Tea. Té. *tay*.

692. Veal (Cutlet). (Chuleta de) ternera. *(choo-LAY-ta day) tayr-NAY-rah*.

693. Bacon. Tocino. *toh-SEE-no*.

694. Tomato. Tomate. *toh-MA-tay*.

695. Grapefruit. Toronja. *toh-ROHN-ha*.

696. Cake. Torta. *TOR-ta*.

697. Omelet or corn griddle cake (*Mex.*). Tortilla. *tor-TEE-yah*.

698. Toast. Tostada. *tohss-TA-da*.

699. Trout. Trucha. *TROO-cha*.

700. Nougat. Turrón. *too-RROHN*.

701. Grapes. Uvas. *OO-vahss*.

702. Venison. Venado. *vay-NA-doh*.

703. Green leafy vegetables.   Verduras.
vayr-DOO-rahss.

704. Carrots.   Zanahorias.   *sah-na-OHR-yahss.*

CHURCH AND RECREATION

LA IGLESIA Y LOS PASATIEMPOS

Church   La iglesia

708. Is there a synagogue?
¿Hay sinagoga?
I see-na-GO-gah?

709. Where is the nearest Catholic church?

¿Dónde está la iglesia católica más cercana?
*DOHN-day ess-TA la ee-GLAY-syah ka-TOH-
lee-ka mahss sayr-KA-na?*

710. We wish to attend an Anglican service.

Queremos asistir a un servicio anglicano.
*kay-RAY-mohss ah-seess-TEER ah oon sayr-VEE-
syo ahn-glee-KA-no.*

711. Where is there a service in English?

¿Dónde predican en inglés?
DOHN-day pray-DEE-kahn en een-GLAYSS?

712. For Baptists, for Methodists.

Para bautistas, para metodistas.
*PA-rah bout-EESS-tahss, PA-rah may-toh-DEESS-
tahss.*

713. For Presbyterians.

Para presbiterianos.
PA-rah press-bee-tay-RYAH-nohss.

714. I want a priest (a minister).

Quiero hablar con un cura (un ministro).
KYAY-ro ah-BLAHR kohn oon KOO-rah (oon mee-NEESS-tro).

715. When is the service (mass)?

¿A qué hora es el servicio (la misa)?
ah kay O-rah ess el sayr-VEE-syo (la MEE-sah)?

716. Is there an English speaking priest?

¿Hay algún cura que hable inglés?
I ahl-GOON KOO-rah kay AH-blay een-GLAYSS?

Sightseeing   Visitas a puntos de interés

721. I want a guide who speaks English.

Deseo un guía que hable inglés.
day-SAY-o oon GHEE-ah kay AH-blay een-GLAYSS.

722. What do you charge an hour (a day)?

¿Cuánto cobra usted por hora (al día)?
KWAHN-toh KO-bra oos-TED por O-rah (ahl DEE-ah)?

723. I am interested in archeology.

Me interesa la arqueología.
may een-tay-RAY-sah la ahr-kay-o-lo-HEE-ah.

724. Native arts and crafts.

Las artes y obras indígenas.
lahss AHR-tess ee O-brahss een-DEE-hay-nahss.

725. Painting, ruins.

La pintura, las ruinas.
la peen-TOO-rah, lahss RRWEE-nahss.

726. Sculpture.

La escultura.
la ess-kool-TOO-rah.

727. I shall have time to visit the museums.

Tendré tiempo de visitar los museos.
ten-DRAY TYEM-po day vee-see-TAR lohss moo-SAY-ohss.

728. The cathedral.

La catedral.
la ka-tay-DRAHL.

729. The bull ring.

La plaza de toros.
la PLAH-sah day TOH-rohss.

730. The library, the monastery.

La biblioteca, el monasterio.
la bee-blee-o-TAY-ka, el mo-nahss-TAY-ryo.

731. The park, the palace.

El parque, el palacio.
el PAR-kay, el pa-LA-syo.

732. Is it open (still)?

¿Está abierta (todavía)?
ess-TA ah-BYAYR-ta (toh-da-VEE-ah)?

733. How long does it stay open?

¿Hasta qué hora está abierto?
AHSS-ta kay O-rah ess-TA ah-BYAYR-toh?

734. How long must we wait?

¿Cuánto tiempo tenemos que esperar?
KWAHN-toh TYEM-po tay-NAY-mohss kay ess-pay-RAHR?

735. Where is the entrance (exit)?

¿Dónde está la entrada (la salida)?
DOHN-day ess-TA la en-TRA-da (la sah-LEE-da)?

736. What is the entrance fee?

¿Cuánto se paga por entrar?
KWAHN-toh say PA-gah por en-TRAHR?

737. Do we need a guide?

¿Necesitamos un guía?
nay-say-see-TA-mohss oon GHEE-ah?

738. How much is the catalog (guide book)?

¿Cuánto cuesta el catálogo (la guía)?
KWAHN-toh KWESS-ta el ka-TA-lo-go (la GHEE-ah)?

739. May I take photographs?

¿Se permite sacar fotografías?
say payr-MEE-tay sah-KAR fo-toh-grah-FEE-ahss?

740. Do you sell postcards (souvenirs)?

¿Vende postales (recuerdos)?
VEN-day pohss-TA-less (rray-KWAYR-dohss)?

741. Have you a book in English about ——?

¿Tiene un libro en inglés sobre ——?
TYAY-nay oon LEE-bro en een-GLAYSS SO-bray ——?

742. Take me back to the hotel now.

Lléveme al hotel ahora.
YAY-vay-may ahl o-TEL ah-O-rah.

743. Go back by way of ——.

Regrese por ——.
rray-GRAY-say por ——.

Amusements   Las diversiones

748. What is there to do today?

¿Qué diversiones hay para hoy?
kay dee-vayr-SYO-ness I PA-rah oy?

749. A bull fight, a concert.

Una corrida de toros, un concierto.
OO-na ko-RREE-da day TOH-rohss, oon kohn-SYAYR-toh.

750. Movies, native dances.

Cine, bailes populares.
SEE-nay, BY-less po-poo-LA-ress.

751. The beach, the pool.

La playa, la piscina.
la PLAH-yah, la peess-SEE-na.

752. Tennis (courts), golf (course).

El (campo de) tenis, el (campo de) golf.
el (KAHM-po day) TAY-neess, el (KAHM-po day) golf.

753. A night club, the opera, the theater.

Un cabaret, la ópera, el teatro.
oon ka-ba-RET, la O-pay-rah, el tay-AH-tro.

754. Is there a matinée today?

¿Hay función esta tarde?
I foon-SYOHN ESS-ta TAR-day?

755. When does the performance start?

¿A qué hora comienza la función?
ah kay O-rah ko-MYEN-sah la foon-SYOHN?

756. The floor show is at about 10.

Se presenta la revista a eso de las diez.
say pray-SEN-ta la rray-VEESS-ta ah AY-so day lahss dyess.

757. Cover charge, minimum.

El precio de admisión, el mínimo.
el PRAY-syo day ahd-mee-SYOHN, el MEE-nee-mo.

758. Where can we go to dance?

¿Adónde podemos ir a bailar?
ah-DOHN-day po-DAY-mohss eer ah by-LAHR?

759. What should I wear?

¿Qué clase de traje debo llevar?
kay KLAH-say day TRA-hay DAY-bo yay-VAHR?

760. Have you any seats for tonight?

¿Hay asientos para esta noche?
I ah-SYEN-tohss PA-rah ESS-ta NO-chay?

761. An orchestra seat, reserved seat.

Una butaca, un asiento reservado.
OO-na boo-TA-ka, oon ah-SYEN-toh rray-sayr-VAH-doh.

762. In the balcony, a box.

En el anfiteatro; un palco.
en el ahn-fee-tay-AH-tro, oon PAHL-ko.

763. The checkroom, the usher.

El vestuario, el acomodador.
el vess-TWAH-ryo, el ah-ko-mo-da-DOR.

764. Can I see (hear) well from there?

¿Puedo ver (oír) bien desde allí?
PWAY-doh vayr (o-EER) byen DEZ-day ah-YEE?

765. Not too near (far).

No muy cerca (lejos).
no mwee SAYR-ka (LAY-hohss).

766. The music is excellent.

La música es excelente.
la MOO-see-ka ess ex-say-LEN-tay.

767. This is very entertaining (funny).

Esto es muy divertido (cómico).
ESS-toh ess mwee dee-vayr-TEE-doh (KO-mee-ko).

768. May I have this dance?

¿Me permite esta pieza?
may payr-MEE-tay ESS-ta PYAY-sah?

SHOPPING AND PERSONAL SERVICES

LAS COMPRAS Y LOS SERVICIOS

772. I want to go shopping.
Deseo ir de compras.
day-SAY-o eer day KOHM-prahss.

773. Where is there a bakery?

¿Dónde hay una panadería?
DOHN-day I OO-na pa-na-day-REE-ah?

774. A candy store, a cigar store.

Una dulcería, una cigarrería.
OO-na dool-say-REE-ah, OO-na see-gah-rray-REE-ah.

775. A clothing store, a department store.
Una tienda de ropas, un almacén.
OO-na TYEN-da day RRO-pahss, oon ahl-ma-SEN.

776. A drug store, a grocery.
Una farmacia, una tienda de comestibles.
OO-na far-MA-syah, OO-na TYEN-da day ko-mess-TEE-bless.

777. A hardware store.
Una ferretería.
OO-na fay-rray-tay-REE-ah.

778. A hat shop, a jewelry store.
Una sombrerería, una joyería.
OO-na sohm-bray-ray-REE-ah, OO-na ho-yay-REE-ah.

779. A market, a shoe store.
Un mercado, una zapatería.
oon mayr-KA-doh, OO-na sah-pa-tay-REE-ah.

780. A tailor shop.
Una sastrería.
OO-na sahss-tray-REE-ah.

781. Shoe (watch) repairs.
Reparación de zapatos (de reloj).
rray-pa-rah-SYOHN day sah-PA-tohss (day rray-LOH).

Also see CLOTHING, p. 84, and COMMON OBJECTS, p. 113.

782. Sale; bargain sale.

Venta; ganga *or* baratillo.
VEN-ta; GAHN-gah or ba-rah-TEE-yo.

783. I want to buy ——.

Quiero comprar ——.
KYAY-ro kohm-PRAHR ——.

784. I (do not) like this.

(No) me gusta esto.
(no) may GOOSS-ta ESS-toh.

785. How much is that?

¿Cuánto es eso?
KWAHN-toh ess AY-so?

786. I prefer something better (cheaper).

Prefiero algo mejor (más barato).
pray-FYAY-ro AHL-go may-HOR (mahss ba-RAH-toh).

787. Please show me some samples.

Favor de mostrarme unas muestras.
fah-VOR day mohss-TRAHR-may OO-nahss MWAY-strahs.

788. It is too large (small).

Es muy grande (pequeño).
ess mwee GRAHN-day (pay-KAY-nyo).

789. Show me some others.

Muéstreme otros.
MWESS-tray-may O-trohss.

790. It does not fit.

No me queda bien.
no may KAY-da byen.

791. Can I order one?

¿Puedo mandar hacer uno?
PWAY-doh mahn-DAHR ah-SAYR OO-no?

792. How long will it take?

¿Cuánto tardará?
KWAHN-toh tar-da-RAH?

793. Please take my measurements.

Haga el favor de tomarme las medidas.
*AH-gah el fah-VOR day toh-MAR-may lahss may-
DEE-dahss.*

794. May I try this on?

¿Me permite probarme esto?
may payr-MEE-tay pro-BAR-may ESS-toh?

795. Will you wrap this, please?

Hágame el favor de envolver esto.
*AH-gah-may el fah-VOR day en-vohl-VAYR ESS-
toh.*

796. It is not becoming.

No me va bien.
no may vah byen.

797. Whom do I pay?

¿A quién pago?
ah kyen PA-go?

798. Pack this for shipment to ——.

Empaque esto para embarcar a ——.
em-PA-kay ESS-toh PA-rah em-bar-KAR ah ——.

Post Office. El correo

804. Where is the post office?

¿Dónde está el correo?
DOHN-day ess-TA el ko-RRAY-o?

805. A post card (a letter) to —— ?

¿Una tarjeta postal (una carta) para —— ?
OO-na tar-HAY-ta pohss-TAHL (OO-na KAR-ta)
PA-rah ——?

806. I want five stamps of —— centavos.

Deseo cinco estampillas de —— centavos.
day-SAY-o SEEN-ko ess-tahm-PEE-yahss day ——
sen-TA-vohss.

807. How many stamps do I need?

¿Cuántas estampillas necesito?
KWAHN-tahss ess-tahm-PEE-yahss nay-say-SEE-
toh?

808. There is nothing dutiable in this.

No hay nada sujeto a impuesto en esto.
no I NA-da soo-HAY-toh ah eem-PWESS-toh en
ESS-toh.

809. Will this go out today?

¿Saldrá esto hoy?
sahl-DRAH ESS-toh oy?

810. Give me a receipt, please.

Déme un recibo, por favor.
DAY-may oon rray-SEE-bo, por fah-VOR.

811. I want to send a money order.

Quiero mandar un giro postal.
KYAY-ro mahn-DAHR oon HEE-ro pohss-TAHL.

812. To which window do I go?

¿A qué ventanilla voy?
ah kay ven-ta-NEE-yah voy?

813. By air mail, by parcel post.

Por correo aéreo, por paquete postal.
*por ko-RRAY-o ah-AY-ray-o, por pa-KAY-tay
pohss-TAHL.*

814. Registered, special delivery.

Certificado, entrega inmediata.
*sayr-tee-fee-KA-doh, en-TRAY-gah een-may-
DYAH-ta.*

815. Insured.

Asegurado.
ah-say-goo-RAH-doh.

Bank   El banco

819. Where is the nearest bank?

¿Dónde está el banco más cercano?
*DOHN-day ess-TA el BAHN-ko mahss sayr-KA-
no?*

820. At which window do I cash this?

¿En qué ventanilla puedo cobrar esto?
*en kay ven-ta-NEE-yah PWAY-doh ko-BRAHR
ESS-toh?*

821. Can you change this for me?

¿Puede usted cambiarme esto?
PWAY-day oos-TED kahm-BYAHR-may ESS-toh?

822. Will you cash a check?

¿Quiere usted cobrarme un cheque?
KYAY-ray oos-TED ko-BRAHR-may oon CHAY-kay?

823. (Do not) give me large bills, please.

Favor de (no) darme billetes grandes.
fah-VOR day (no) DAHR-may bee-YAY-tess GRAHN-dess.

824. May I have small change?

¿Puede usted darme cambio?
PWAY-day oos-TED DAHR-may KAHM-byo?

825. I have a letter of credit.

Tengo una carta de crédito.
TEN-go OO-na KAR-ta day KRAY-dee-toh.

826. What is the exchange rate on the dollar?

¿A cómo está el cambio del dólar?
ah KO-mo ess-TA el KAHM-byo del DOH-lahr?

827. Travelers' checks, a draft.

Cheques para viajeros, un giro.
CHAY-kess PA-rah vyah-HAY-rohss, oon HEE-ro.

Bookstore and Stationer's

La librería y la papelería

831. Where is there a bookstore?

¿Dónde hay una librería?
DOHN-day I OO-na lee-bray-REE-ah?

832. A stationer's, a news stand.

Una papelería, un puesto de periódicos.
*OO-na pa-pay-lay-REE-ah, oon PWESS-toh day
pay-RYO-dee-kohss.*

833. Newspapers, magazines.

Periódicos, revistas.
pay-RYO-dee-kohss, rray-VEESS-tahss.

834. A dictionary, a guide book.

Un diccionario, una guía.
oon deek-syo-NA-ryo, OO-na GHEE-ah.

835. A map of ——.

Un mapa de ——.
oon MA-pa day ——.

836. Playing cards, post cards.

Naipes, tarjetas postales.
NY-pess, tar-HAY-tahss pohss-TA-less.

837. Greeting cards.

Tarjetas de saludos.
tar-HAY-tahss day sah-LOO-dohss.

838. Carbon paper.

Papel carbón.
pa-PELL kar-BONE.

839. Writing paper, ink.

Papel para cartas, tinta.
pa-PELL PA-rah KAR-tahss, TEEN-ta.

840. Envelopes (for air mail), a pencil.

Sobres (para correo aéreo), un lápiz.
SO-bress (PA-rah ko-RRAY-o·ah-AY-ray-o), oon LA-pees.

841. A fountain pen, artist's materials.

Una pluma fuente, artículos para pintores.
OO-na PLOO-ma FWEN-tay, ahr-TEE-koo-lohss PA-rah peen-TOH-ress.

842. (Strong) string, an eraser.

Cuerda (fuerte), una goma para borrar.
KWAYR-da (FWAYR-tay), OO-na GO-ma PA-rah bo-RRAHR.

843. Typewriter ribbon.

Cinta para máquina.
SEEN-ta PA-rah MA-kee-na.

844. Tissue paper, wrapping paper.

Papel de seda, papel para envolver.
pa-PELL day SAY-da, pa-PELL PA-rah en-vohl-VAYR.

Cigar Store   La tabaquería

849. Where is the nearest cigar store?

¿ Dónde está la tabaquería más cercana?
DOHN-day ess-TA la ta-ba-kay-REE-ah mahss sayr-KA-na?

850. I want some cigars.

> Deseo unos cigarros or puros.
> *day-SAY-o OO-nohss see-GAH-rrohss or POO-rohss.*

851. A pack of cigarettes, please.

> Un paquete de cigarrillos, por favor.
> *oon pa-KAY-tay day see-gah-RREE-yohss, por fah-VOR.*

852. I need a lighter.

> Necesito un encendedor.
> *nay-say-SEE-toh oon en-sen-day-DOR.*

853. Flints, fluid.

> Piedras de encendedor, líquido.
> *PYAY-drahss day en-sen-day-DOR, LEE-kee-doh.*

854. Matches, a pipe.

> Fósforos, una pipa.
> *FOSS-fo-rohss, OO-na PEE-pa.*

855. Pipe tobacco, a pouch.

> Tabaco, una bolsa para tabaco.
> *ta-BAH-ko, OO-na BOHL-sah PA-rah ta-BAH-ko.*

Barber Shop and Beauty Parlor

La peluquería y el salón de belleza

860. Where is there a good barber?

> ¿Dónde hay un buen peluquero?
> *DOHN-day I oon bwen pay-loo-KAY-ro?*

861. I want a haircut (a shave).

Quisiera que me cortara el pelo (una afeitada).
*kee-STAY-rah kay may kor-TAR-rah el PAY-lo
(OO-na ah-fay-TA-da).*

862. Not very short.

No muy corto.
no mwee KOR-toh.

863. Do not cut any off the top.

No corte de arriba.
no KOR-tay day ah-RREE-ba.

864. At the back and sides.

De atrás y de los lados.
day ah-TRAHSS ee day lohss LA-dohss.

865. (Do not) put on oil.

(No) me ponga pomada.
(no) may POHN-gah po-MA-da.

866. I part my hair on the (other) side.

Me hago la raya al (otro) lado.
may AH-go la RRAH-yah ahl (O-tro) LA-doh.

867. In the middle.

En medio.
en MAY-dyo.

868. The water is too hot (cold).

El agua está muy caliente (fría).
*el AH-gwa ess-TA mwee ka-LYEN-tay
(FREE-ah).*

869. I want my shoes shined.

Quiero hacerme lustrar los zapatos.
KYAY-ro ah-SAYR-may looss-TRAHR lohss sah-PA-tohss.

870. Can I make an appointment for ——?

¿Puedo hacer una cita para ——?
PWAY-doh ah-SAYR OO-na SEE-ta PA-rah ——?

871. I wish a shampoo and set.

Deseo un shampoo y peinado.
day-SAY-o oon shahm-POO ee pay-NA-doh.

872. A finger wave.

Un peinado al agua.
oon pay-NA-doh ahl AH-gwa.

873. A permanent wave.

Una permanente.
OO-na payr-ma-NEN-tay.

874. A facial, a manicure.

Un masaje, un manicure.
oon ma-SAH-hay, oon ma-nee-KOO-ray.

Photography   La fotografía

879. I want a roll of (color) film.

Quiero un rollo de película (de color).
KYAY-ro oon RRO-yo day pay-LEE-koo-la (day ko-LOHR).

880. The size is ——.

El tamaño es ——.
el ta-MA-nyo ess ——.

881. Movie film, for this camera.

Un rollo de película de cine, para esta cámara.
*oon RRO-yo day pay-LEE-koo-la day SEE-nay,
PA-rah ESS-ta KA-ma-rah.*

882. What is the charge for developing a roll?

¿Cuánto cuesta revelar un rollo?
*KWAHN-toh KWESS-ta rray-vay-LAHR oon
RRO-yo?*

883. For one print of each.

Por una copia de cada negativo.
por OO-na KO-pyah day KA-da nay-gah-TEE-vo.

884. For an enlargement.

Por una ampliación.
por OO-na ahm-plee-ah-SYOHN.

885. My camera is out of order.

Mi cámara está descompuesta.
mee KA-ma-rah ess-TA dess-kohm-PWESS-ta.

886. When will they be ready?

¿Cuándo estarán listas?
KWAHN-doh ess-ta-RAHN LEESS-tahss?

887. Do you rent cameras?

¿Se alquilan cámaras?
say ahl-KEE-lahn KA-ma-rahss?

888. I should like one for today.

> Quisiera una para hoy.
> *kee-SYAY-rah OO-na PA-rah oy.*

Laundry and Dry Cleaning

La lavandería y la tintorería

893. Where is the nearest laundry (dry cleaner)?

> ¿Dónde está la lavandería (la tintorería) más cercana?
> *DOHN-day ess-TA la la-vahn-day-REE-ah (la teen-toh-ray-REE-ah) mahss sayr-KA-na?*

894. I have something to be washed.

> Tengo algo para hacer lavar.
> *TEN-go AHL-go PA-rah ah-SAYR la-VAHR.*

895. Pressed (brushed, mended).

> Para hacer planchar (cepillar, remendar).
> *PA-rah ah-SAYR plahn-CHAHR (say-pee-YAHR, rray-men-DAHR).*

896. For the dry cleaner.

> Para la tintorería.
> *PA-rah la teen-toh-ray-REE-ah.*

897. Do not wash this in hot water.

> No lave esto en agua caliente.
> *no LA-vay ESS-toh en AH-gwa ka-LYEN-tay.*

898. Use lukewarm water.

> Use agua tibia.
> *OO-say AH-gwa TEE-byah.*

899. Be very careful.

Tenga mucho cuidado.
TEN-gah MOO-cho kwee-DA-doh.

900. Do not dry this in the sun.

No ponga esto al sol.
no POHN-gah ESS-toh ahl sohl.

901. Do not starch the collars.

No almidone los cuellos.
no ahl-mee-DOH-nay lohss KWAY-yohss.

902. When can I have this?

¿Cuándo puedo tener esto?
KWAHN-doh PWAY-doh tay-NAYR ESS-toh?

903. Here is the list.

Aquí tiene usted la lista.
ah-KEE TYAY-nay oos-TED la LEESS-ta.

904. The belt is missing.

Falta el cinturón.
FAHL-ta el seen-too-ROHN.

Clothing   Los vestidos

909. Apron, bathing cap.

El delantal, el gorro de baño.
el day-lahn-TAHL, el GO-rro day BA-nyo.

910. Bathing suit, blouse.

El traje de baño, la blusa.
el TRA-hay day BA-nyo, la BLOO-sah.

911. Brassiere, coat (suit).

El sostén, el saco.
el sohss-TEN, el SAH-ko.

912. Collar, diapers.

El cuello, los pañales.
el KWAY-yo, lohss pa-NYAH-less.

913. Dress, garters.

El vestido, las ligas.
el vess-TEE-doh, lahss LEE-gahss.

914. Gloves, handkerchief.

Los guantes, el pañuelo.
lohss GWAHN-tess, el pa-NWAY-lo.

915. Hat, jacket.

El sombrero, la chaqueta.
el sohm-BRAY-ro, la cha-KAY-ta.

916. Necktie, nightgown.

La corbata, el camisón.
la kor-BA-ta, el ka-mee-SOHN.

917. Overcoat, pajamas.

El abrigo, la pijama.
el ah-BREE-go, la pee-HAH-ma.

918. Panties; petticoat.

Los calzones; el refajo or el fondo.
*lohss kahl-SO-ness; el rray-FAH-ho or el FOHN-
doh.*

919. Robe, shirt.

La bata, la camisa.
la BA-ta, la ka-MEE-sah.

920. Raincoat, riding clothes.

El impermeable, el traje de montar.
el eem-payr-may-AH-blay, el TRA-hay day mohn-TAR.

921. Shorts, skirt.

Los calzoncillos, la falda.
lohss kahl-sohn-SEE-yohss, la FAHL-da.

922. Slip, slippers.

La combinación, las zapatillas.
la kohm-bee-nah-SYOHN, lahss sah-pa-TEE-yahss.

923. Socks, stockings.

Los calcetines, las medias.
lohss kahl-say-TEE-ness, lahss MAY-dyahss.

924. Suit, suspenders.

El traje, los tirantes.
el TRA-hay, lohss tee-RAHN-tess.

925. Sweater, trousers.

El suéter, los pantalones.
el SWAY-tayr, lohss pahn-ta-LO-ness.

926. Undershirt, underwear.

La camiseta, la ropa interior.
la ka-mee-SAY-ta, la RRO-pa een-tay-RYOR.

927. Vest.

El chaleco.
el chah-LAY-ko.

HEALTH   LA SALUD

Accidents   Los accidentes

Also see ILLNESS, p. 90.

932. There has been an accident.

Hubo un accidente.
OO-bo oon ahk-see-DEN-tay.

933. Get a doctor (nurse).

Llame a un doctor (una enfermera).
YAH-may ah oon dohk-TOHR (OO-na en-fayr-
MAY-rah).

934. Send for an ambulance.

Mande buscar una ambulancia.
MAHN-day booss-KAR OO-na ahm-boo-LAHN-
syah.

935. Please bring blankets.

Por favor, traiga unas frazadas.
por fah-VOR, TRY-gah OO-nahss frah-SAH-
dahss.

936. A stretcher, water.

Una camilla, agua.
OO-na ka-MEE-yah, AH-gwa.

937. He is (seriously) hurt.

Está (gravemente) herido.
ess-TA (grah-vay-MEN-tay) ay-REE-doh.

938. Help me carry him.

Ayúdeme a cargarlo.
ay-YOO-day-may ah kar-GAHR-lo.

939. He was knocked down.

Fué atropellado.
fway ah-tro-pay-YAH-doh.

940. She has fallen (fainted).

Ella se cayó (se desmayó).
AY-yah say ka-YO (say dess-ma-YO).

941. I feel faint.

Me estoy desmayando.
may ess-TOY dess-ma-YAHN-doh.

942. He has a fracture (bruise, cut).

Tiene una fractura (una contusión, una herida).
TYAY-nay OO-na frahk-TOO-rah (OO-na kohn-too-SYOHN, OO-na ay-REE-da).

943. He has burned his hand.

Se quemó la mano.
say kay-MO la MA-no.

944. It is bleeding (swollen).

Está sangrando (hinchado).
ess-TA sahn-GRAHN-doh (een-CHA-doh).

945. Can you dress this?

¿Puede usted curar esto?
PWAY-day oos-TED koo-RAHR ESS-toh?

946. Have you any bandages (a splint)?

¿Tiene usted vendajes (una tablilla)?
TYAY-nay oos-TED ven-DA-hess (OO-na ta-BLEE-yah)?

947. I need something for a tourniquet.

Necesito algo para un torniquete.
nay-say-SEE-toh AHL-go PA-rah oon tor-nee-KAY-tay.

948. Are you all right?

¿Está usted bien?
ess-TA oos-TED byen?

949. It hurts here.

Me duele aquí.
may DWAY-lay ah-KEE.

950. I want to sit down a moment.

Quiero sentarme un momento.
KYAY-ro sen-TAR-may oon mo-MEN-toh.

951. I cannot move my ——.

No puedo mover mi ——.
no PWAY-doh mo-VAYR mee ——.

952. I have hurt my ——.

Me lastimé el ——.
may lahss-tee-MAY el ——.

See PARTS OF THE BODY, p. 100.

953. Can I travel on Monday?

¿Puedo viajar el lunes?
PWAY-doh vyah-HAHR el LOO-ness?

954. Please notify my husband (my wife).

Sírvase avisar a mi marido (mi esposa).
*SEER-vah-say ah-vee-SAHR ah mee ma-REE-doh
(mee ess-PO-sah).*

955. Here is my identification.

Aquí tiene usted mi carnet de identificación.
*ah-KEE TYAY-nay oos-TED mee kar-NET day
ee-den-tee-fee-ka-SYOHN.*

Illness   La enfermedad

Also see ACCIDENTS, p. 87.

960. I wish to see a doctor.

Deseo ver a un doctor.
day-SAY-o vayr ah oon dohk-TOHR.

961. A specialist, an American doctor.

Un especialista, un médico norteamericano.
*oon ess-pay-syah-LEESS-ta, oon MAY-dee-ko nor-
tay-ah-may-ree-KA-no.*

962. I do not sleep well.

No duermo bien.
no DWAYR-mo byen.

963. My foot hurts.

Me duele el pie.
may DWAY-lay el pyay.

964. My head aches.

Tengo dolor de cabeza.
TEN-go doh-LOHR day ka-BAY-sah.

965. I have an abscess.

Tengo un absceso.
TEN-go oon ahb-SAY-so.

966. Appendicitis, biliousness.

Apendicitis, ataque de bilis.
ah-pen-dee-SEE-teess, ah-TA-kay day BEE-leess.

967. A bite (insect), a blister.

Una picadura, una ampolla.
OO-na pee-ka-DOO-rah, OO-na ahm-PO-yah.

968. A boil, a burn.

Un divieso, una quemadura.
oon dee-VYAY-so, OO-na kay-ma-DOO-rah.

969. Chills, a cold.

Escalofríos, un catarro.
ess-ka-lo-FREE-ohss, oon ka-TA-rro.

970. Constipation, a cough.

Estreñimiento, una tos.
ess-tray-nyee-MYEN-toh, OO-na tohss.

971. A cramp, diarrhoea, dysentery.

Un calambre, diarrea, disentería.
*oon ka-LAHM-bray, dyah-RRAY-ah, dee-sen-tay-
REE-ah.*

972. Earache, fever.

Dolor de oído, calentura.
doh-LOHR day o-EE-doh, ka-len-TOO-rah.

973. Food poisoning, a headache.

Envenenamiento, dolor de cabeza.
en-vay-nay-na-MYEN-toh, doh-LOHR day ka-BAY-sah.

974. Hoarseness, indigestion.

Una ronquera, indigestión.
OO-na rrohn-KAY-rah, een-dee-hess-TYOHN.

975. Nausea, pneumonia.

Náuseas, pulmonía.
NOW-say-ahss, pool-mo-NEE-ah.

976. A sore throat, a sprain.

Inflamación de la garganta, una torcedura.
een-flah-ma-SYOHN day la gahr-GAHN-ta, OO-na tor-say-DOO-rah.

977. A sting, sunburn.

Una picadura, quemadura de sol.
OO-na pee-ka-DOO-rah, kay-ma-DOO-rah day sohl.

978. Sunstroke, typhoid fever.

Insolación, fiebre tifoidea.
een-so-la-SYOHN, FYAY-bray tee-foy-DAY-ah.

979. Vomiting.

Vómitos.
VO-mee-tohss.

980. What am I to do?

¿Qué debo hacer?
kay DAY-bo ah-SAYR?

981. Must I stay in bed?

¿Tengo que guardar cama?
TEN-go kay gwahr-DAHR KA-ma?

982. Do I have to go to the hospital?

¿Tengo que ir al hospital?
TEN-go kay eer ahl ohss-pee-TAHL?

983. May I get up?

¿Puedo levantarme?
PWAY-doh lay-vahn-TAR-may?

984. I feel better.

Me siento mejor.
may SYEN-toh may-HOR.

985. When do you think I'll be better?

¿Cuándo cree usted que me sentiré mejor?
KWAHN-doh KRAY-ay oos-TED kay may sen-tee-RAY may-HOR?

986. When will you come again?

¿Cuándo vuelve usted?
KWAHN-doh VWELL-vay oos-TED?

987. A drop (liquid).

Una gota.
OO-na GO-ta.

988. A tablespoonful, a teaspoonful.

Una cucharada, una cucharadita.
OO-na koo-cha-RAH-da, OO-na koo-cha-rah-DEE-ta.

989. Every hour (3 hours).

Cada hora (tres horas).
KA-da O-rah (trayss O-rahss).

990. Before (after) meals.

Antes (después) de las comidas.
AHN-tess (dess-PWESS) day lahss ko-MEE-dahss.

991. Twice a day.

Dos veces al día.
dohss VAY-sess ahl DEE-ah.

992. On going to bed, getting up.

Al acostarse, al levantarse.
ahl ah-kohss-TAR-say, ahl lay-vahn-TAR-say.

993. X-ray.

Una radiografía.
OO-na rrah-dyo-grah-FEE-ah.

See also DRUG STORE, p. 95.

Dentist   El dentista

999. Where is there a good dentist?

¿Dónde hay un buen dentista?
DOHN-day I oon bwen den-TEESS-ta?

1000. This tooth hurts.

Me duele este diente.
may DWAY-lay ESS-tay DYEN-tay.

1001. Can you fix it (temporarily)?

¿Puede usted componerlo (por ahora)?
PWAY-day oos-TED kohm-po-NAYR-lo (por ah-O-rah)?

1002. I have lost a filling.

Perdí una tapadura.
payr-DEE OO-na ta-pa-DOO-rah.

1003. I have broken a tooth.

Me rompí un diente.
may rrohm-PEE oon DYEN-tay.

1004. I do not want it extracted.

No deseo que lo saque.
no day-SAY-o kay lo SAH-kay.

1005. Can you repair this denture?

¿Puede usted componer esta dentadura?
PWAY-day oos-TED kohm-po-NAYR ESS-ta den-ta-DOO-rah?

1006. Local anesthetic.

Un anestésico local.
oon ah-ness-TAY-see-ko lo-KAHL.

Drugstore La farmacia

1012. Where is a drugstore where they speak English?

¿Dónde hay una farmacia donde se hable inglés?
DOHN-day I OO-na far-MA-syah DOHN-day say AH-blay een-GLAYSS?

1013. Can you fill this prescription?
¿Puede prepararme esta receta?
PWAY-day pray-pa-RAHR-may ESS-ta rray-SAY-ta?

1014. How long will it take?
¿Cuánto tiempo tardará?
KWAHN-toh TYEM-po tar-da-RAH?

1015. I want adhesive tape.
Quiero esparadrapo.
KYAY-ro ess-pa-rah-DRAH-po.

1016. Alcohol, analgesic.
Alcohol, analgésico.
ahl-ko-OHL, ah-nahl-HAY-see-ko.

1017. An antiseptic, aspirin.
Un antiséptico, aspirina.
oon ahn-tee-SEP-tee-ko, ahss-pee-REE-na.

1018. Bandages, bicarbonate of soda.
Vendas, bicarbonato de soda.
VEN-dahss, bee-kar-bo-NA-toh day SO-da.

1019. Boric acid.
Ácido bórico.
AH-see-doh BO-ree-ko.

1020. A brush (hair, tooth).
Un cepillo (de cabeza, de dientes).
oon say-PEE-yo (day ka-BAY-sah, day DYEN-tess).

1021. Cleaning fluid.
Un quitamanchas.
oon kee-ta-MAHN-chahss.

1022. Carbolic acid, castor oil.

Ácido fénico, aceite de ricino.
AH-see-do FAY-nee-ko, ah-SAY-tay day rree-SEE-no.

1023. Chlorine tablets for water.

Píldoras de cloro para el agua.
PEEL-doh-rahss day KLO-ro PA-rah el AH-gwa.

1024. Cold cream, a comb.

Crema para la cara, un peine.
KRAY-ma PA-rah la KA-rah, oon PAY-nay.

1025. Corn pads, cotton.

Parches para los callos, algodón.
PAR-chess PA-rah lohss KA-yohss, ahl-go-DOHN.

1026. A depilatory, a deodorant.

Un depilatorio, un desodorante.
oon day-pee-la-TOH-ryo, oon dess-o-doh-RAHN-tay.

1027. Ear stoppers.

Tapones para el oído.
ta-PO-ness PA-rah el o-EE-doh.

1028. Epsom salts.

Sal inglesa.
sahl een-GLAY-sah.

1029. Foot powder.

Talco para los pies.
TAHL-ko PA-rah lohss pyayss.

1030. Gauze, hair tonic.

Gasa, loción para el pelo.
GAH-sah, lo-SYOHN PA-rah el PAY-lo.

1031. A hot water bottle, an ice bag.

Una botella para agua caliente, un saquito
para hielo.
*OO-na bo-TAY-yah PA-rah AH-gwa ka-LYEN-
tay, oon sah-KEE-toh PA-rah YAY-lo.*

1032. Insect bite (lotion), insect repellent.

Picadura (loción para), insecticida.
*pee-ka-DOO-rah (lo-SYOHN PA-rah), een-sek-
tee-SEE-da.*

1033. Iodine, a laxative.

Yodo, un laxante.
YO-doh, oon lak-SAHN-tay.

1034. A lipstick, a medicine dropper.

Un lápiz de labios, un gotero.
oon LA-peess day LA-byohss, oon go-TAY-ro.

1035. A mouth wash.

Un gargarismo.
oon gahr-gah-REESS-mo.

1036. Peroxide, poison.

Agua oxigenada, veneno.
AH-gwa ok-see-hay-NAH-da, vay-NAY-no.

1037. Powder, quinine.

Polvos, quinina.
POHL-vohss, kee-NEE-na.

1038. A razor, razor blades.

Una navaja de afeitar, hojas de afeitar.
*OO-na na-VAH-ha day ah-fay-TAR, O-hahss
day ah-fay-TAR.*

1039. Rouge.

Colorete.
ko-lo-RAY-tay.

1040. Sanitary napkins, a sedative.

Toallas higiénicas, un sedante.
*toh-AH-yahss ee-HYAY-nee-kahss, oon say-
DAHN-tay.*

1041. Shampoo (cream, liquid).

(Crema, líquido) para el shampoo.
*(KRAY-ma, LEE-kee-doh) PA-rah el shahm-
POO.*

1042. Shaving cream (lotion).

Crema(loción) de afeitar.
KRAY-ma (lo-SYOHN) day ah-fay-TAR.

1043. Soap, sunburn ointment.

Jabón, ungüento para quemadura de sol.
*ha-BOHN, oon-GWEN-toh PA-rah kay-ma-
DOO-rah day sohl.*

1044. Sun tan lotion.

Loción contra quemadura de sol.
*lo-SYOHN KOHN-tra kay-ma-DOO-rah day
sohl.*

1045. A thermometer.

Un termómetro.
oon tayr-MO-may-tro.

1046. Tooth paste (powder).
Pasta (polvos) para los dientes.
PAHSS-ta (POHL-vohss) PA-rah lohss DYEN-tess.

Parts and Organs of the Body

Las partes y los órganos del cuerpo

1052. The ankle.   El tobillo.   *el toh-BEE-yo.*

1053. The appendix.   El apéndice.
el ah-PEN-dee-say.

1054. The arm.   El brazo.   *el BRA-so.*

1055. The back.   La espalda.   *la ess-PAHL-da.*

1056. The blood.   La sangre.   *la SAHN-gray.*

1057. The bone.   El hueso.   *el WAY-so.*

1058. The cheek.   La mejilla.   *la may-HEE-yah.*

1059. The chest.   El pecho.   *el PAY-cho.*

1060. The chin.   La barba.   *la BAR-ba.*

1061. The collarbone.   La clavícula.
la klah-VEE-koo-la.

1062. The ear.   La oreja.   *la o-RAY-ha.*

1063. The elbow.   El codo.   *el KO-doh.*

1064. The eye.   El ojo.   *el O-ho.*

1065. The eyebrow.   La ceja.   *la SAY-ha.*

1066. The eyelash.   La pestaña.   *la pess-TA-nyah.*

1067. The eyelid.   El párpado.   *el PAR-pa-doh.*

1068. The face.   La cara.   *la KA-rah.*

1069. The finger.   El dedo.   *el DAY-doh.*

1070. The foot.   El pie.   *el pyay.*

1071. The forehead.   La frente.   *la FREN-tay.*

1072. The hair.   El pelo.   *el PAY-lo.*

1073. **The hand.** La mano. *la MA-no.*

1074. **The head.** La cabeza. *la ka-BAY-sah.*

1075. **The heart.** El corazón. *el ko-rah-SOHN.*

1076. **The heel.** El talón. *el ta-LOHN.*

1077. **The hip.** La cadera. *la ka-DAY-rah.*

1078. **The intestines.** Los intestinos.
lohss een-tess-TEE-nohss.

1079. **The jaw.** La mandíbula.
la mahn-DEE-boo-la.

1080. **The joint.** La coyuntura.
la ko-yoon-TOO-rah.

1081. **The kidney.** El riñón. *el rree-NYOHN.*

1082. **The knee.** La rodilla. *la rro-DEE-yah.*

1083. **The leg.** La pierna. *la PYAYR-na.*

1084. **The lip.** El labio. *el LA-byo.*

1085. **The liver.** El hígado. *el EE-gah-doh.*

1086. **The lung.** El pulmón. *el pool-MOHN.*

1087. **The mouth.** La boca. *la BO-ka.*

1088. **The muscle.** El músculo.
el MOOSS-koo-lo.

1089. **The nail (finger, toe).** La uña.
la OO-nyah.

1090. **The neck.** El cuello. *el KWAY-yo.*

1091. **The nerve.** El nervio. *el NAYR-vyo.*

1092. **The nose.** La nariz. *la na-REESS.*

1093. **The rib.** La costilla. *la kohss-TEE-yah.*

1094. **The shoulder.** El hombro. *el OHM-bro.*

1095. **The (left, right) side.**
El costado (izquierdo, derecho).
el kohss-TA-doh (eess-KYAYR-doh, day-RAY-cho).

1096. **The skin.** La piel. *la pyell.*

1097. The skull. El cráneo. *el KRAH-nay-o.*

1098. The spine. La espina. *la ess-PEE-na.*

1099. The stomach. El estómago.
el ess-TOH-ma-go.

1100. The tooth. El diente. *el DYEN-tay.*

1101. The tendon. El tendón. *el ten-DOHN.*

1102. The thigh. El muslo. *el MOOZ-lo.*

1103. The throat. La garganta.
la gahr-GAHN-ta.

1104. The thumb. El pulgar. *el pool-GAHR.*

1105. The toe. El dedo del pie.
el DAY-doh del pyay.

1106. The tongue. La lengua. *la LEN-gua.*

1107. The tonsils. Las amígdalas.
lahss ah-MEEG-da-lahss.

1108. The waist. La cintura. *la seen-TOO-rah.*

1109. The wrist. La muñeca. *la moo-NYAY-ka.*

COMMUNICATIONS

LAS COMUNICACIONES

Telephone   El teléfono

See NUMBERS, p. 109.

1115. Where may I telephone?
¿Dónde puedo telefonear?
DOHN-day PWAY-doh tay-lay-fo-nay-AHR?

1116. Will you telephone for me?
¿Quiere telefonear de mi parte?
KYAY-ray tay-lay-fo-nay-AHR day mee PAR-tay?

1117. I want to make a local call to ——.
Deseo hacer una llamada a ——.
day-SAY-o ah-SAYR OO-na yah-MA-da ah ——.

1118. A long distance call.
Una llamada de larga distancia.
OO-na yah-MA-da day LAHR-gah deess-TAHN-syah.

1119. The operator will call you.
La telefonista le llamará.
la tay-lay-fo-NEESS-ta lay yah-ma-RAH.

1120. I want number ——.
Quiero el número ——.
KYAY-ro el NOO-may-ro ——.

1121. Hello.
Aló *or* Bueno.
ah-LO or BWAY-no.

1122. They do not answer.
No contestan.
no kohn-TESS-tahn.

1123. The line is busy.
La línea está ocupada.
la LEE-nay-ah ess-TA o-koo-PA-da.

1124. Dial it again.
Llame otra vez.
YAH-may O-tra vess.

1125. May I speak to ——.
Deseo hablar con ——.
day-SAY-o ah-BLAHR kohn ——.

1126. He is not in.
Él no está.
el no ess-TA.

1127. This is —— speaking.
Habla ——.
AH-bla ——.

1128. Please take a message for ——.
Haga el favor de tomar un mensaje para ——.
AH-gah el fah-VOR day toh-MAR oon men-SAH-hay PA-rah ——.

1129. My number is ——.
Mi número de teléfono es ——.
mee NOO-may-ro day tay-LAY-fo-no ess ——.

1130. How much is a call to ——?
¿Cuánto cuesta llamar a ——?
KWAHN-toh KWESS-ta yah-MAR ah ——?

1131. You have a telephone call.
Le llaman por teléfono.
lay YAH-mahn por tay-LAY-fo-no.

Telegrams and Cablegrams

Los telegramas y los cablegramas

1137. Where can I send a telegram (a cable)?
¿Dónde puedo poner un telegrama (un cablegrama)?
DOHN-day PWAY-doh po-NAYR oon tay-lay-GRAH-ma (oon ka-blay-GRAH-ma)?

1138. What is the rate a word to ——?
¿Cuánto por palabra a ——?
KWAHN-toh por pa-LA-bra ah ——?

1139. Where are the forms?
¿Dónde están las formas?
DOHN-day ess-TAHN lahss FOR-mahss?

1140. Urgent, collect.
    Urgente, por cobrar.
    oor-HEN-tay, por ko-BRAHR.

1141. When will it arrive?
    ¿Cuándo llegará?
    KWAHN-doh yay-gah-RAH?

1142. I wish to pay for the answer.
    Quiero pagar la respuesta.
    KYAY-ro pa-GAHR la rress-PWESS-ta.

USEFUL INFORMATION
INFORMES UTILES

Days of the week

Los días de la semana

1148. Monday, Tuesday.
    Lunes, martes.
    LOO-ness, MAR-tess.

1149. Wednesday, Thursday.
    Miércoles, jueves.
    mee-AYR-ko-less, hoo-AY-vess.

1150. Friday, Saturday.
    Viernes, sábado.
    vee-AYR-ness, SAH-ba-doh.

1151. Sunday.
    Domingo.
    doh-MEEN-go.

Months, Seasons, the Weather
Los meses, las estaciones, el tiempo

1152. January, February.
    Enero, febrero.
    ay-NAY-ro, fay-BRAY-ro.

1153. March, April.
Marzo, abril.
MAR-so, ah-BREEL.

1154. May, June.
Mayo, junio.
MA-yo, HOO-nyo.

1155. July, August.
Julio, agosto.
HOO-lyo, ah-GOHSS-toh.

1156. September, October.
Septiembre, octubre.
sep-tee-EM-bray, ok-TOO-bray.

1157. November, December.
Noviembre, diciembre.
no-vee-EM-bray, dee-see-EM-bray.

1158. Spring, Summer.
La primavera, el verano.
la pree-ma-VAY-rah, el vay-RAH-no.

1159. Autumn, Winter.
El otoño, el invierno.
el o-TOH-nyo, el een-vee-AYR-no.

1160. It is warm (cold).
Hace calor (frío).
AH-say ka-LOHR (FREE-o).

1161. It is fair (bad).
Hace sol (mal tiempo).
AH-say sohl (mahl TYEM-po).

1162. It is raining.
Llueve.
yoo-AY-vay.

1163. The sun, sunny, shady.
El sol, asoleado, sombreado.
el sohl, ah-so-lay-AH-doh, sohm-bray-AH-doh.

Time and Time Expressions   La hora, etc.

1169. What time is it?
¿Qué hora es?   *kay O-rah ess?*

1170. It is one o'clock.
Es la una.   *ess la OO-na.*

1171. It is half past five.
Son las cinco y media.
sohn lahss SEEN-ko ee MAY-dyah.

1172. It is a quarter past five.
Son las cinco y cuarto.
sohn lahss SEEN-ko ee KWAHR-toh.

1173. It is a quarter to six.
Son las seis menos cuarto.
sohn lahss sayss MAY-nohss KWAHR-toh.

1174. At ten past seven (in the morning).
A las siete y diez (de la mañana).
ah lahss SYAY-tay ee dyess (day la ma-NYAH-na).

1175. At ten to nine (in the evening).
A las nueve menos diez (de la noche).
ah lahss NWAY-vay MAY-nohss dyess (day la NO-chay).

1176. It is late.
Ya es tarde.   *yah ess TAR-day.*

1177. In the afternoon.
Por la tarde.   *por la TAR-day.*

1178. In the morning (evening).
Por la mañana (la noche).
por la ma-NYAH-na (la NO-chay).

1179. Day, night.
El día, la noche.
el DEE-ah, la NO-chay.

1180. At noon, at midnight.
A mediodía, a media noche.
ah may-dyo-DEE-ah, ah MAY-dyah NO-chay.

1181. Yesterday, last night.
Ayer, anoche.
ah-YAYR, ah-NO-chay.

1182. Today, tonight.
Hoy, esta noche.
oy, ESS-ta NO-chay.

1183. Tomorrow.
Mañana.
ma-NYAH-na.

1184. (The) day before yesterday.
Anteayer.
ahn-tay-ah-YAYR.

1185. Last year (month).
El año (el mes) pasado.
el AH-nyo (el mess) pa-SAH-doh.

1186. Last Monday.
El lunes pasado.
el LOO-ness pa-SAH-doh.

1187. Next week.
La semana próxima.
la say-MA-na PROHK-see-ma.

1188. Two weeks ago.
Hace dos semanas.
AH-say dohss say-MA-nahss.

1190. Numbers   Los números
One, two, three.
Uno, dos, tres.
OO-no, dohss, trayss.

Four, five, six.
Cuatro, cinco, seis.
KWAH-tro, SEEN-ko, sayss.

Seven, eight, nine.
Siete, ocho, nueve.
SYAY-tay, O-cho, NWAY-vay.

Ten, eleven, twelve.
Diez, once, doce.
dyess, OHN-say, DOH-say.

Thirteen, fourteen.
Trece, catorce.
TRAY-say, ka-TOR-say.

Fifteen, sixteen.
Quince, diez y seis.
KEEN-say, dyess ee sayss.

Seventeen, eighteen.
Diez y siete, diez y ocho.
dyess ee SYAY-tay, dyess ee O-cho.

Nineteen, twenty.
Diez y nueve, veinte.
dyess ee NWAY-vay, VAYN-tay.

Twenty-one, twenty-two.
Veinte y uno, veinte y dos.
VAYN-tay ee OO-no, VAYN-tay ee dohss.

Thirty, thirty-one.
Treinta, treinta y uno.
TRAYN-ta, TRAYN-ta ee OO-no.

Forty, fifty.
Cuarenta, cincuenta.
kwah-REN-ta, seen-KWEN-ta.

Sixty, seventy.
Sesenta, setenta.
say-SEN-ta, say-TEN-ta.

Eighty, ninety.
Ochenta, noventa.
o-CHEN-ta, no-VEN-ta.

One hundred, one hundred one.
Cien, ciento uno.
syen, SYEN-toh OO-no.

Two hundred, three hundred.
Doscientos, Trescientos.
dohss-SYEN-tohss, trayss-SYEN-tohss.

Four hundred, five hundred.
Cuatrocientos, quinientos.
kwah-tro-SYEN-tohss, kee-NYEN-tohss.

Six hundred, seven hundred.
Seiscientos, setecientos.
sayss-SYEN-tohss, say-tay-SYEN-tohss.

Eight hundred, nine hundred.
Ochocientos, novecientos.
o-cho-SYEN-tohss, no-vay-SYEN-tohss.

One thousand, two thousand.
Mil, dos mil.
meel, dohs meel.

First, second.
Primero, segundo.
pree-MAY-ro, say-GOON-doh.

Third, fourth.
Tercero, cuarto.
tayr-SAY-ro, KWAHR-toh.

Fifth, sixth.
Quinto, sexto.
KEEN-toh, SEX-toh.

Seventh, eighth.
Séptimo, octavo.
SEP-tee-mo, ok-TA-vo.

Ninth, tenth.
Noveno, décimo.
no-VAY-no, DAY-see-mo.

Measurements　　Las medidas

1191. What is the length (width)?
¿Qué largo (ancho) tiene?
kay LAHR-go (AHN-cho) TYAY-nay?

1192. How much per meter?
¿Cuánto por metro?
KWAHN-to por MAY-tro?

1193. What is the size?
¿De qué tamaño es?
day kay ta-MA-nyo ess?

1194. It is ten meters long by four meters wide.
Tiene diez metros de largo por cuatro metros de ancho.
TYAY-nay dyess MAY-trohss day LAHR-go por KWAH-tro MAY-trohss day AHN-cho.

1195. Large, small, medium.
Grande, pequeño, mediano.
GRAHN-day, pay-KAY-nyo, may-DYAH-no.

1196. High, low.
  Alto, bajo.
  AHL-toh, BA-ho.

1197. Alike, different.
  Igual, diferente.
  ee-GWAHL, dee-fay-REN-tay.

1198. A pair, a dozen.
  Un par, una docena.
  oon par, OO-na doh-SAY-na.

1199. Half a dozen.
  Media docena.
  MAY-dyah doh-SAY-na.

1200. Half a meter.
  Medio metro.
  MAY-dyoh MAY-tro.

Colors   Los colores

1205. Light, dark.
  Claro, oscuro.
  KLAH-ro, ohss-KOO-ro.

1206. Black, blue, brown.
  Negro, azul, café *or* marrón.
  NAY-gro, ah-SOOL, kah-FAY or *ma-RROHN.*

1207. Cream, gray, green.
  Crema, gris, verde.
  KRAY-ma, greess, VAYR-day.

1208. Orange, pink, purple.
  Anaranjado, rosado, morado.
  ah-na-rahn-HA-doh, rro-SAH-doh, mo-RAH-doh.

1209. Red, white.
  Rojo, blanco.
  RRO-ho, BLAHN-ko.

1210. Yellow. Amarillo. *ah-ma-REE-yo.*

1211. I want a lighter (darker) shade.
Quiero un tono más claro (más oscuro).
KYAY-ro oon TOH-no mahss KLAH-ro (mahss ohss-KOO-ro).

Common Objects. Objetos ordinarios

1217. Ash tray. El cenicero. *el say-nee-SAY-ro.*

1218. Bag. El saco. *el SAH-ko.*

1219. Bobby pins. Las horquillas.
lahss or-KEE-yahss.

1220. Box. La caja. *la KA-ha.*

1221. Bulb (light). La bombilla.
la bohm-BEE-yah.

1222. Candy. Los dulces. *lohss DOOL-sess.*

1223. Can opener. El abrelatas.
el ah-bray-LA-tahss.

1224. Cloth (cotton). La tela (de algodón).
la TAY-la (day ahl-go-DOHN).

1225. Corkscrew. El tirabuzón.
el tee-rah-boo-SOHN.

1226. Cushion. El cojín. *el ko-HEEN.*

1227. Doll. La muñeca. *la moo-NYAY-ka.*

1228. Earring. El arete. *el ah-RAY-tay.*

1229. Flashlight. La linterna eléctrica.
la leen-TAYR-na ay-LEK-tree-ka.

1230. Glasses (sun). Los lentes (oscuros).
lohss LEN-tess (ohss-KOO-rohss).

1231. Gold. El oro. *el O-ro.*

1232. Gum (chewing). El chicle. *el CHEE-klay.*

1233. Hairnet. La redecilla. *la rray-day-SEE-yah.*

1234. Hairpin. La horquilla. *la or-KEE-yah.*

1235. Hook. El ganchito. *el gahn-CHEE-toh.*

1236. Iron (flat). La plancha. *la PLAHN-cha.*

1237. Jewelry. Las joyas. *lahss HO-yahss.*

1238. Lace (shoe). La cinta de zapatos.
la SEEN-ta day sah-PA-tohss.

1239. Leather. El cuero. *el KWAY-ro.*

1240. Linen. De lino. *day LEE-no.*

1241. Mending cotton. El hilo para remiendos.
el EE-lo PA-rah rray-MYEN-dohss.

1242. Mosquito net. El mosquitero.
el mohss-kee-TAY-ro.

1243. Nail file. La lima de uñas.
la LEE-ma day OO-nyahss.

1244. Necklace. El collar. *el ko-YAHR.*

1245. Needle. La aguja. *la ah-GOO-ha.*

1246. Notebook. La libreta. *la lee-BRAY-ta.*

1247. Padlock. El candado. *el kahn-DA-doh.*

1248. Pail. El balde *or* el cubo.
el BAHL-day or el KOO-bo.

1249. Penknife. El cortaplumas.
el kor-ta-PLOO-mahss.

1250. Perfume. El perfume. *el payr-FOO-may.*

1251. Pin (ornamental). El broche.
el BRO-chay.

1252. Pin (straight). El alfiler. *el ahl-fee-LAYR.*

1253. Radio (radio broadcast).
El radio (la radio).
el RRAH-dyo (la RRAH-dyo).

1254. Rayon. De rayón. *day rrah-YOHN.*

1255. Ring. El anillo. *el ah-NEE-yo.*

1256. Rubbers. Los zapatos de hule.
lohss sah-PA-tohss day OO-lay.

1257. Safety pin.
El imperdible *or* el alfiler de seguridad.
*el eem-payr-DEE-blay or el ahl-fee-LAYR day
say-goo-ree-DAHD.*

1258. Scissors. Las tijeras. *lahss tee-HAY-rahss.*

1259. Silk. De seda . *day SAY-da.*

1260. Silver. La plata. *la PLAH-ta.*

1261. Stone (precious). La piedra (preciosa).
la PYAY-drah (pray-SYO-sah).

1262. Stopper. El tapón. *el ta-POHN.*

1263. Strap. La correa. *la ko-RRAY-ah.*

1264. Straw. La paja. *la PA-ha.*

1265. Thimble. El dedal. *el day-DAHL.*

1266. Thread. El hilo. *el EE-lo.*

1267. Toy. El juguete. *el hoo-GAY-tay.*

1268. Typewriter. La máquina de escribir.
la MA-kee-na day ess-kree-BEER.

1269. Umbrella. El paraguas.
el pa-RAH-gwahss.

1270. Vase. El florero. *el flo-RAY-ro.*

1271. Wash cloth. El trapo. *el TRA-po.*

1272. Watch (wrist). El reloj (de pulsera).
el rray-LOH (day pool-SAY-rah).

1273. Whiskbroom. La escobilla.
la ess-ko-BEE-yah.

1274. Wire (metal). El alambre.
el ah-LAHM-bray.

1275. Wood. La madera.   *la ma-DAY-rah.*

1276. Wool (cloth). De lana.   *day LA-na.*

1277. Wool (mending). El hilo de lana.
el EE-lo day LA-na.

1278. Zipper. El cierre de corredera.
el STAY-rray day ko-rray-DAY-rah.

METRIC CONVERSION TABLES
LENGTH

1 centimetro (cm.) = 2/5 in.
1 metro (m.) = 100 cms. = 39 in.
1 kilómetro (km.) = 1,000 m. = 5/8 mile.
1 in. = $2\frac{1}{2}$ cms.
1 ft. = 30 cms.
1 yd. = 90 cms.

WEIGHT

1 gramo = .036 oz.
100 gramos = $3\frac{1}{2}$ oz.
1 kilo = (1,000 gramos) = 2 lbs. 2 oz.
1 oz. = 28 gramos.
1 lb. = 453 gramos.

CAPACITY

1 pint = .47 litro.
1 quart = .95 litro.
1 gallon = 3.76 litros.

NATIVE FOOD AND DRINK LIST

This food supplement consists mainly of native Spanish dishes. We have however also included a selection of Latin American, South American and Mexican dishes; all of which show strong Spanish influence. All foods have been alphabetized according to Spanish to facilitate menu reading. Typical and standard American foods can be found in the restaurant section of the text.

Note that dining hours in Spain, Latin and South America are distinctly later than they are in the United States. Breakfast is simple, usually rolls and coffee served between 8–11 a.m. Lunch is leisurely and substantial; usually served between 1–3 o'clock and always followed by a siesta. Dinner or supper is customarily served after 9 p.m. and more likely after 10 o'clock. The custom of stopping at 5 o'clock for cocktails or coffee and a snack is very characteristic of Spanish life. It is typical of Spanish night life to begin extremely late and to continue far into the night.

SOPAS: SOUPS
APERTIVOS: APPETIZERS

Calderada. Fish soup; a variety of bouillabaisse.

Caldo. Chicken broth.

Caldo de pimentón. Pepper soup.

Entremeses. Hors d'œuvres.

Espárragos. Large, succulent asparagus.

Fondos de alcachofas. Hearts of artichokes with oil and vinegar.

Gazpacho. Chilled vegetable soup made with cucumbers, tomatoes, red pepper, onions, garlic, bread crumbs, oil and vinegar.

Potaje de garbanzos. Pea soup made with chick peas.

Potaje de habas secas. Bean soup made with dried beans.

Salmorejo. Chilled vegetable soup similar to Gazpacho.

Sancochas de camerones. Shrimp chowder.

Sopa de Agriao. Potato and watercress soup.

Sopa de ajo. Garlic soup usually served with a poached egg.

Sopa de ajo blanco con uvas. Garlic soup with grapes.

Sopa de albóndigas. Soup with meat balls made with a tomato base and served with small fried meat balls in it.

Sopa de almendras. Purée of almond soup.

Sopa de camarones. Shrimp soup.

Sopa de coles. Cabbage soup.

Sopa de cuarto de hora. Fish soup made of fish and shell fish and served with hard boiled eggs, peas and toasted bread.

Sopa de galápagos.   Turtle soup.
Sopa de legumbres.   Vegetable soup.
Sopa de mariscos.   Seafood soup.
Sopa de ostras.   Oyster soup.
Sopa de pan con gambas.   Bread soup with prawns.
Sopa de pescado.   Fish soup prepared with one kind of fish or a variety of native fish.
Sopa de puchero.   Thick beef soup.
Sopa de rana.   Frog soup.
Sopa de tomate.   Tomato soup.
Sopa de verduras.   Vegetable soup.
Sopa española.   Soup made with rice, tomatoes, peppers and spices.
Tapas.   Small snacks taken with sherry or vermouth before meals consisting of olives, almonds, cheese, fish, anchovies.

PESCADO: FISH
MARISCOS: SHELLFISH

Abadejo.   Cod.
Alli-pebre d'anguiles.   Eel in garlic sauce.
Almejas.   Clams.
Almejas con arroz.   Clams and rice.
Anguilas.   Eels.
Arenques.   Herring.
Atún.   Tuna fish.
Atún en escabeche.   Pickled tuna.
Bacalao.   Dried cod fish.
Besugo.   Sea bream.
Bogavante.   Lobster.
Bonito.   Bonito.

Boquerones. Fish, very much like anchovies.

Caballa. Mackerel.

Calamares. Squid.

Calamares en su tinta. Small cuttlefish simmered in their own ink.

Caldereta asturiana. Mixed fish stew.

Callos. Tripe.

Camarones. Shrimps.

Cangrejos. Crabs.

Caracoles. Snails.

Chanquetes. Small, thin fried fish.

Chocos con habas. Cuttlefish with broad beans.

Chupe. Thick fish stew.

Coquines. Cockles.

Escabeche. Pickled fish.

Gambas. Large shrimp.

Huachinango. Red snapper.

Lamprea. Lamprey.

Langosta. Variety of lobster.

Langostinos. Shellfish (crayfish) similar to shrimp.

Lenguado. Sole.

Lentejas con chorizo. Lentils and sausage.

Lisa. Grey mullet.

Llobarro, grillé o hervido. Sea bass, grilled or boiled.

Mariscos. Shellfish.

Marmita. Fish stew in which bonito is predominant.

Mejillones. Mussels.

Merluza. Codfish.

Mítulos rellenos. Stuffed mussels.

Ostras. Oysters.

Paella. Popular Spanish dish prepared with chicken, shellfish, sausage, pimento and saffron-flavored rice.

Paella de mariscos. Rice and seafood.

Pargo encebollado.   Red bream baked with onions.
Perca.   Perch.
Pescado blanco en ajillo.   White fish with garlic.
Pescado con arroz.   Fish with rice.
Pescado con salsa de coconut.   Fish with a coconut sauce.
Pez espada en amarillo.   Swordfish cooked with herbs.
Raya en pimentón.   Skate and red pepper.
Róbalo.   Bass.
Rodaballo.   Flounder.
Rollo de pescado.   Fish roll.
Sábalo.   Shad.
Salmón.   Salmon.
Salmonetes.   Baby salmon.
Sardinas.   Sardines.
Trucha.   Trout.
Zarzuela.   Mixture of seafoods prepared in a spicy sauce.

CARNE: MEAT   AVES: POULTRY
ESPECIALIDADES: SPECIALTIES

Ajiaco.   Meat, chicken, pepper, avocado and potatoes prepared in a stew.
Ajoqueso.   Latin American dish of melted cheese and peppers.
Albondigón.   Meat loaf.
Arroz con pollo.   Chicken with rice.
Arroz a la parellada.   Rice prepared with chicken, meat and vegetables.
Biftec or bistec.   Steak.
Berenjena rellena.   Stuffed eggplant.

Butifarra.   Pork sausage.

Cabeza de ternera.   Calf's head with vinaigrette sauce.

Cabrito asado.   Roast leg of spring lamb.

Caldo gallego.   Thick stew of meat and vegetables.

Cazuela de cordero.   Lamb stew made with corn, peas, beans, rice, potatoes and herbs.

Cebollas y frijoles.   Bean-stuffed onions.

Chanfaina.   Goat entrails with vegetables.

Chile con carne.   Highly seasoned ground beef, beans and chile in a spicy sauce.

Chile con queso.   Highly seasoned chili (peppers) and cheese.

Cholupas.   Spicy Mexican dish prepared with sausage, chili and onions.

Chorizo.   Garlic and pork sausage.

Chuletas de cerdo.   Pork cutlets.

Chuletas de cordero.   Lamb cutlets.

Chuletas de ternera.   Veal cutlets.

Cocido.   Boiled meat with ham, bacon, sausage and vegetables.

Cochinillo asado.   Roast suckling pig.

Codornices asadas.   Roast quail.

Cola de vaca.   Oxtail.

Conejo.   Rabbit.

Cordero en ajillo pastor.   Lamb stew.

Corona de cordero.   Crown of lamb.

Costillas de cerdo.   Spareribs.

Costillas de cordero a la parrilla.   Grilled lamb chops.

Croqueta de pollo.   Chicken croquettes.

Croquetas de papas con carne.   Meat and potato cakes.

Empanadas.   Meat pies.

Empanadillas.   Small pastries filled with meat.

Enchiladas. Mexican corn cake stuffed with meat, cheese and chile.

Estofado. Stew made with diced chicken, beef, lamb, ham, onions, tomatoes, herbs and wine.

Fabada asturiana. Pork and beans.

Frijolada. Bean stew with meat and native vegetables.

Frijoles. Beans with bacon and ham.

Fritos de lentejas. Fried lentils.

Fritura mixta. Assorted meat, chicken or fish and vegetables, fried in deep fat.

Gallina. Chicken.

Gallina con garbanzos. Stewed chicken with chick peas.

Guacamole. Finely chopped onions, spices and avocados.

Guisado español. Stew made with beef, onions in olive oil.

Hígado de ternera a la parrilla. Grilled calf's liver.

Humita. Pancake made with fresh corn, tomato, pimento, sugar and oil.

Ignames con ron. Sweet potatoes prepared with rum and sherry.

Jamón. Ham of the region.

Jamón aguadilla. Roast fresh ham.

Jamón serrano. Smoked ham.

Jigote. Meat hash.

Locro. Corn stew made with wheat, meat and spices; popular in South America.

Lomo a la parrilla. Grilled pork chops.

Longaniza. Pork sausage.

Medallones con champiñones. Filet of beef or veal with mushrooms.

Menudo gitana. Well seasoned tripe.

Mole de guajalote. Mexican dish made with chicken, garlic, onions, tomatoes, tortillas in a chocolate sauce.

Mole poblano. Chicken or turkey exotically seasoned and prepared in a chocolate sauce.

Mondongo. Thick stew prepared with many native vegetables.

Morcilla blanca. Sausage made with chicken, bacon, hard boiled eggs and spices.

Morcilla asturiana. Blood sausage.

Olla podrida. Stew made with ham and chick peas.

Paella. Native Spanish dish prepared with chicken, seafood, sausage, onions, garlic, tomatoes, pimento and saffron flavored rice.

Pato con cereza. Braised duck with cherry sauce.

Pato silvestre. Wild duck.

Pavo asado. Roast turkey.

Pecho de ternera. Breast of veal.

Pelota. Chopped beef.

Pepitoria de gallina. Chicken stew made with olives, tomatoes and vegetables.

Perdices asadas. Roast partridge.

Perdiz. Partridge.

Perdiz en escabeche. Marinated partridge.

Picadillo. Hash.

Pichones. Squabs, pigeons.

Pie de cerdo bretóna. Pigs knuckles with beans.

Pierna de cordero. Leg of lamb.

Pimientos rellenos. Stuffed peppers.

Pisto manchego. Stew made with onions, eggs and pork.

Pollo asado frío con ensalada. Chicken salad.

Pollo con naranja. Chicken prepared with an orange sauce.

Pote gallego.   Stew prepared with beef, ham sausage and vegetables.

Puchero.   Boiled dinner made of meat and vegetables.

Puerco estofado.   Spicy, pork stew.

Redondo asado.   Roast veal.

Riñones.   Kidneys.

Riñones al jerez.   Kidneys prepared in a sauce of sherry.

Rollo de Santiago.   Meat loaf covered with potatoes.

Ropa vieja.   Meat hash.

Rosbif.   Roast beef.

Salchichas.   Veal and pork sausage (always eaten fresh).

Salchichón.   Pork and bacon sausage.

Salpicón de ave.   Chicken with mayonnaise.

Sancocho.   Stew of meat, yucca and bananas.

Sesos.   Brains.

Simplón frito.   Fried noodles.

Solomillo.   Filet of veal.

Suculento.   Vegetable dish prepared with corn, squash and other native vegetables.

Tallarines.   Noodles.

Tamale.   A mixture of ground corn filled with minced chicken or meat and steamed or fried in oil.

Ternera asada fría.   Cold roast veal.

Torta de conejo.   Rabbit tart.

Tortas de carne.   Meat patties.

Tortilla, Mexican.   A thin, flat unleavened corn cake.

Tortilla, Spanish.   An omelet.

Tortilla con jamón.   Ham omelet.

Tortilla española.   Spanish omelet.

Tortilla de sardinas.   Sardine omelet.

Tostón asado.   Roast suckling pig.

Tasajo.   Corned beef.

ENSALADAS: SALADS

Ensalada de pepino.   Cucumber salad.
Ensalada de tomate.   Tomato salad.
Ensalada variada.   Mixed green salad.

POSTRES: DESSERTS

Alfajores.   Filled cookies.
Almendrado.   Macaroon.
Arroz con leche.   Rice with milk.
Bizcochitos.   Crackers, cookies.
Bizcochuelo.   Cake.
Budín.   Pudding.
Buñuelos.   Doughnuts.
Cabello de ángel.   Jam made from a gourd, called sidra.
Capirotada.   Sweet pudding made with bread and cinnamon.
Carne de membrillo.   Preserved quince.
Churros.   Light pastry dough rolled into long, thin strips, fried and rolled in sugar.
Compota.   Stewed fruit.
Crema española.   Dessert made of eggs, milk and gelatin.
Cuajada.   Junket.
Flan.   Caramel custard; a classic Spanish dessert.
Flan cremoso.   Boiled custard.
Gelatina.   Gelatin.
Guayaba.   Guava.
Helados.   Ice cream.
Higo en almíbar.   Figs in syrup.
Magdalenas.   Little cakes.
Mantecado.   Ice cream.

Mantecadas de almendras. Almond biscuits.

Masitas. Cupcakes.

Mazapán. Marzipan.

Membrillo. Jellied dessert made of quinces.

Melón. Melon.

Merengue. Meringue.

Migas. Fried bread.

Mostachones. Little cakes eaten at festivities.

Natilla. Custard.

Pastas. Pastry.

Pasteles. Cakes.

Pastelitos. Small cakes.

Perruñas. Little biscuits.

Piña. Pineapple.

Pudín. Pudding.

Roscas. Cookies.

Rosquillas. Biscuits shaped in the form of rings.

Sandía. Watermelon.

Sorbete. Sherbet.

Suspiros. Little fried cakes sprinkled with sugar.

Tarta. Tart, pie.

Tarteletas. Small tarts.

Torta. Cake.

Torta de almendras. Almond tart.

Tortera. Pastry.

Turrón. Nougat dessert.

Yemas. Candy dessert made with egg yolks, sugar, fruits, nuts; formed into small balls.

QUESOS: CHEESES

Cabrales. Somewhat like blue cheese.

Manchego. Spanish cheese made with ewe's milk.

Queso de bola. Cheese made from cow's milk and eaten fresh similar to Dutch edam.

Queso de cabra. Goat's milk cheese.
Queso gallego. Medium soft cheese.
Requesón. Soft, white cheese similar to cottage cheese.

BEBIDAS: DRINKS

Anís. Anise.
Aperitivo. Aperitif.
Cerveza. Beer.
Champaña. Champagne.
Chicha. Fermented maize or pineapple drink.
Coñac. Brandy.
Gaseosa. Soda.
Ginebra. Gin.
Guarapo. Cider.
Jerez. Sherry.
Oporto. Port.
Ponche. Punch.
Pulque. Strong, fermented drink made from the Mexican maquay plant.
Ron. Rum.
Sidra. Cider.
Vino. Wine.
   Vino blanco. White wine.
   Vino de Borgoña. Burgundy wine.
   Vino de Burdeos. Bordeaux wine.
   Vino corriente. Ordinary table wine.
   Vino de cuarte. Pink wine.
   Vino spumoso. Sparkling wine.
   Vino de la tierra. Regional wine.
   Vino tinto. Red wine.

INDEX

The words in capitals refer to sections, and the first number that follows (example: p. 81) refers to the page. Otherwise, ALL ENTRIES ARE INDEXED BY ITEM NUMBER.

LISTEN & LEARN CASSETTES

Complete, practical at-home language learning courses for people with limited study time—specially designed for travelers.

Special features:

* Dual-language—Each phrase first in English, then the foreign-language equivalent, followed by a pause for repetition (allows for easy use of cassette even without manual).

* Native speakers—Spoken by natives of the country who are language teachers at leading colleges and universities.

* Convenient manual—Contains every word on the cassettes—all fully indexed for fast phrase or word location.

Each boxed set contains one 90-minute cassette and complete manual.

Listen & Learn French	Cassette and Manual 99914-9 $8.95
Listen & Learn German	Cassette and Manual 99915-7 $8.95
Listen & Learn Italian	Cassette and Manual 99916-5 $8.95
Listen & Learn Japanese	Cassette and Manual 99917-3 $8.95
Listen & Learn Modern Greek	Cassette and Manual 99921-1 $8.95
Listen & Learn Modern Hebrew	Cassette and Manual 99923-8 $8.95
Listen & Learn Portuguese	Cassette and Manual 99919-X $8.95
Listen & Learn Russian	Cassette and Manual 99920-3 $8.95
Listen & Learn Spanish	Cassette and Manual 99918-1 $8.95
Listen & Learn Swedish	Cassette and Manual 99922-X $8.95

Precise, to-the-point guides for adults with limited learning time

ESSENTIAL GRAMMAR SERIES

Designed for independent study or as supplements to conventional courses, the *Essential Grammar* series provides clear explanations of all aspects of grammar—no trivia, no archaic material. Do not confuse these volumes with abridged grammars. These volumes are complete.

ESSENTIAL FRENCH GRAMMAR, Seymour Resnick. Includes 2500 item cognate list. 159pp. $5\frac{3}{8} \times 8\frac{1}{2}$. •20419-7 Pa. $2.75

ESSENTIAL GERMAN GRAMMAR, Guy Stern and E. F. Bleiler. Unusual shortcuts on noun declension, word order. 124pp. $5\frac{3}{8} \times 8\frac{1}{2}$. •20422-7 Pa. $2.95

ESSENTIAL ITALIAN GRAMMAR, Olga Ragusa. Includes useful discussion of verb idioms essential in Italian. 111pp. $5\frac{3}{8} \times 8\frac{1}{2}$. •20779-X Pa. $2.95

ESSENTIAL JAPANESE GRAMMAR, E. F. Bleiler. In Romaji, no characters needed. Japanese grammar is regular and simple. 156pp. $5\frac{3}{8} \times 8\frac{1}{2}$. 21027-8 Pa. $2.95

ESSENTIAL PORTUGUESE GRAMMAR, Alexander da R. Prista. Includes 4 appendices covering regular, irregular verbs. 114pp. $5\frac{3}{8} \times 8\frac{1}{2}$. 21650-0 Pa. $3.50

ESSENTIAL SPANISH GRAMMAR, Seymour Resnick. Includes 2500 word cognate list. 115pp. $5\frac{3}{8} \times 8\frac{1}{2}$. •20780-3 Pa. $2.75

ESSENTIAL ENGLISH GRAMMAR, Philip Gucker. Combines modern functional and traditional approaches. 177pp. $5\frac{3}{8} \times 8\frac{1}{2}$. 21649-7 Pa. $3.50

•Not available in British Commonwealth Countries except Canada.